MR. STUFFiNS

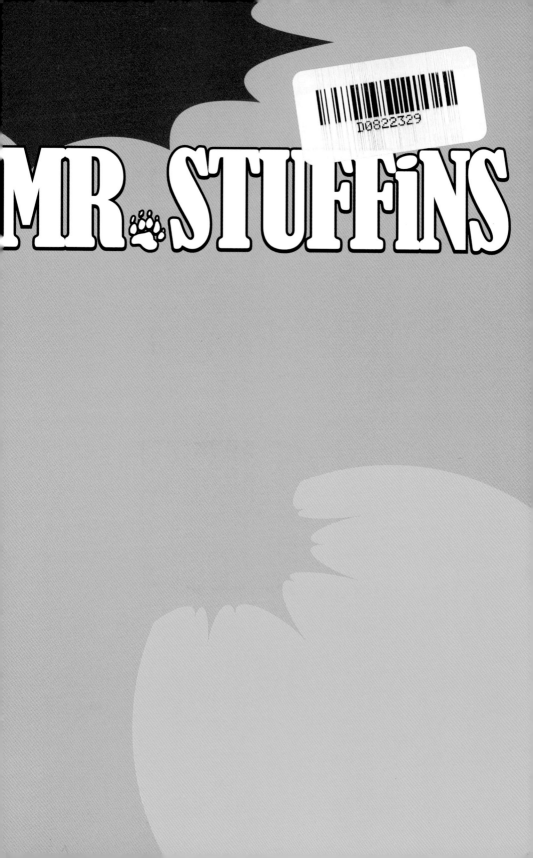

WRITTEN BY
ANDREW COSBY AND JOHANNA STOKES

ROSS RICHIE
chief executive officer

ANDREW COSBY
chief creative officer

MARK WAID
editor-in-chief

ADAM FORTIER
vice president,
publishing

CHIP MOSHER
marketing director

MATT GAGNON
managing editor

MR. STUFFINS - September 2009 published by BOOM! Studios. Mr. Stuffins is copyright © 2009 Boom Entertainment, Inc. BOOM! Studios™ and the BOOM! logo are trademarks of Boom Entertainment, Inc., registered in various countries and categories. All rights reserved. The characters and events depicted herein are fictional. Any similarity to actual persons, demons, anti-Christs, aliens, vampires, face-suckers or political figures, whether living, dead or undead, or toany actual or supernatural events is coincidental and unintentional. So don't come whining to us. Office of publication: 6310 San Vicente Blvd Ste 404, Los Angeles, CA 90048-5457. Printed in Korea.

ART BY
AXEL MEDELLIN MACHAIN

COLORS BY
ANDRES LOZANO AND DANIELA FIORE

LETTERED BY
JOHNNY LOWE

COVER BY
DAVID PETERSEN

EDITED BY
IAN BRILL

CHAPTER ONE

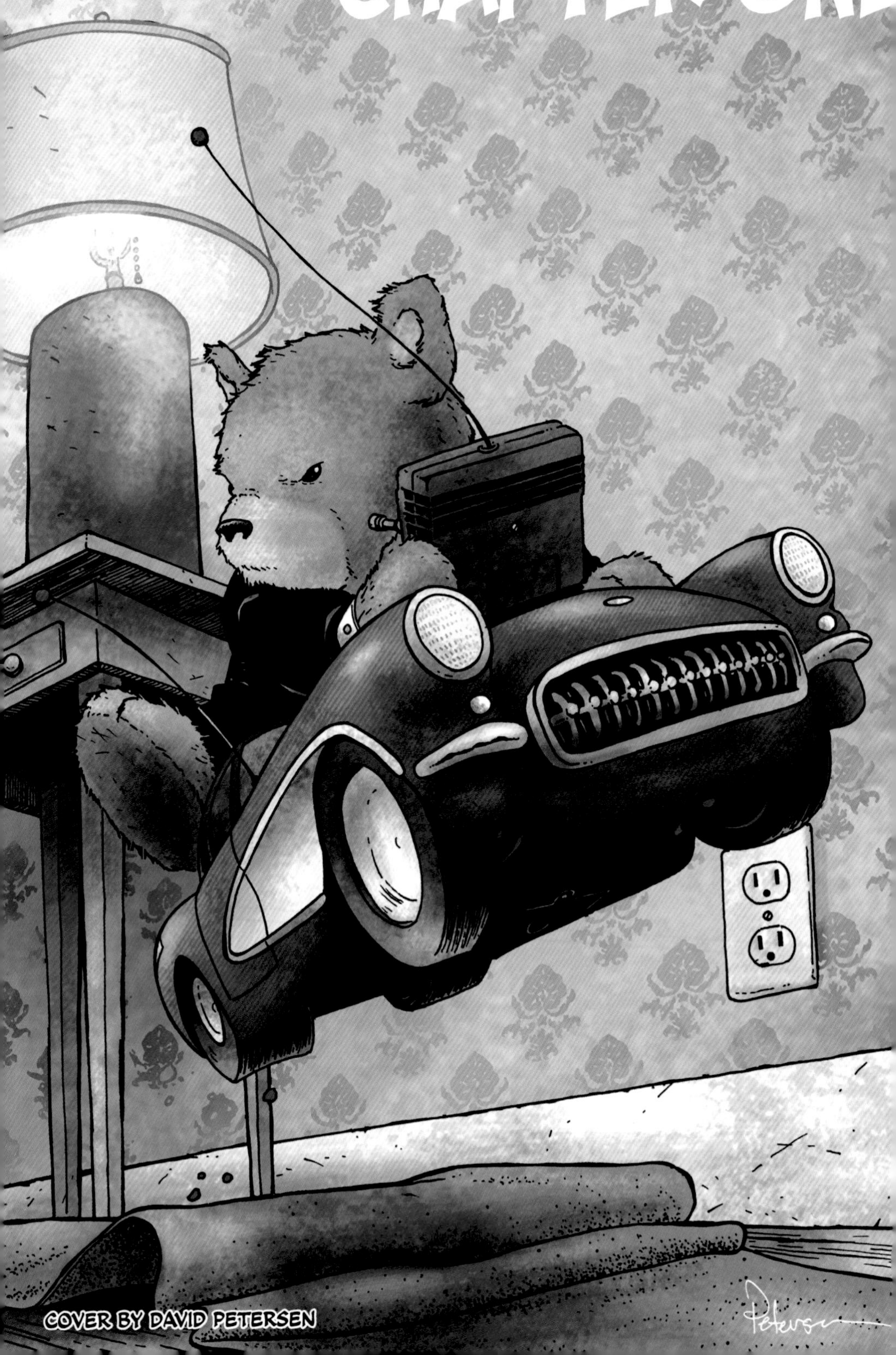

COVER BY DAVID PETERSEN

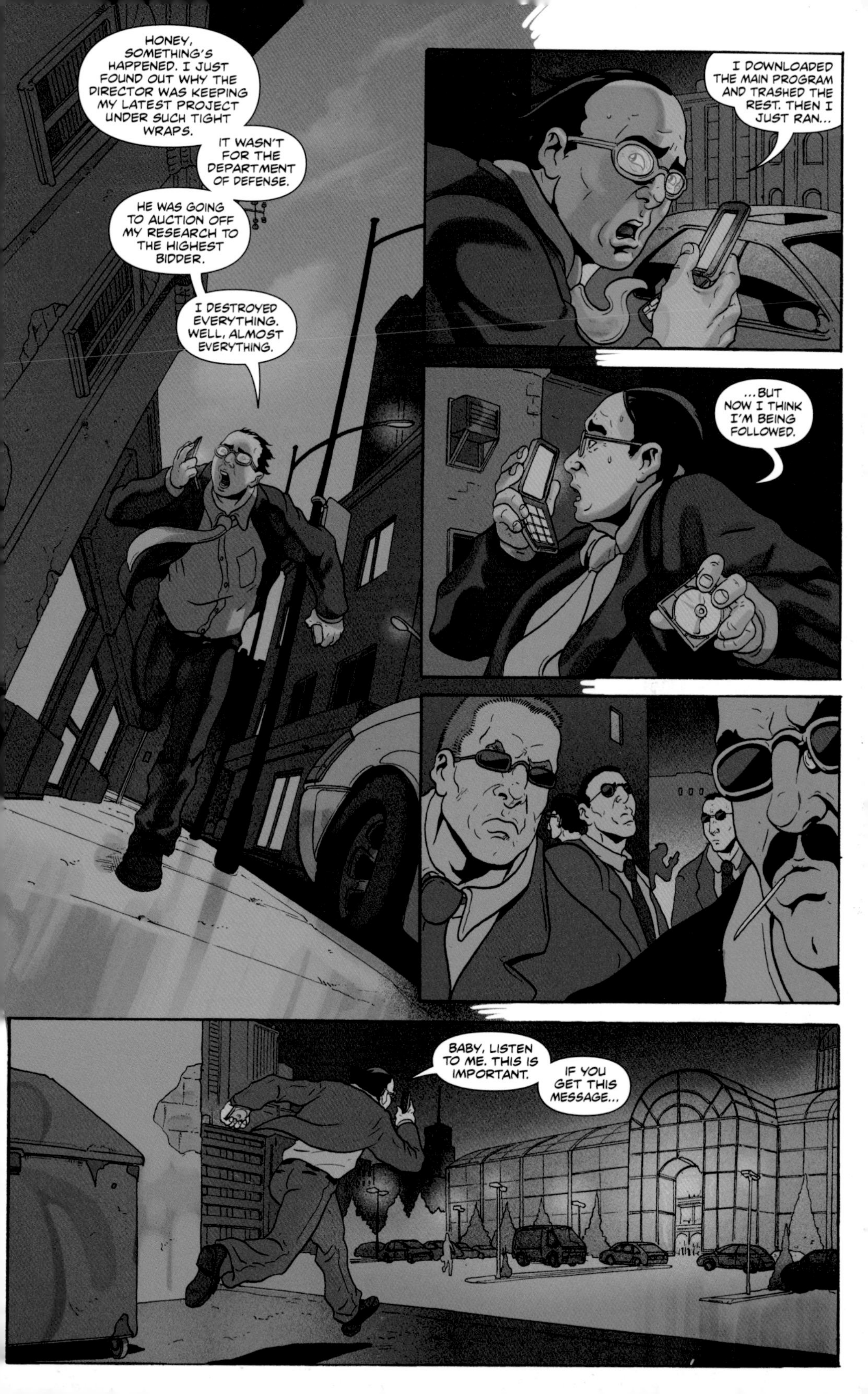
HONEY, SOMETHING'S HAPPENED. I JUST FOUND OUT WHY THE DIRECTOR WAS KEEPING MY LATEST PROJECT UNDER SUCH TIGHT WRAPS.
IT WASN'T FOR THE DEPARTMENT OF DEFENSE.
HE WAS GOING TO AUCTION OFF MY RESEARCH TO THE HIGHEST BIDDER.
I DESTROYED EVERYTHING. WELL, ALMOST EVERYTHING.
I DOWNLOADED THE MAIN PROGRAM AND TRASHED THE REST. THEN I JUST RAN...
...BUT NOW I THINK I'M BEING FOLLOWED.
BABY, LISTEN TO ME. THIS IS IMPORTANT.
IF YOU GET THIS MESSAGE...

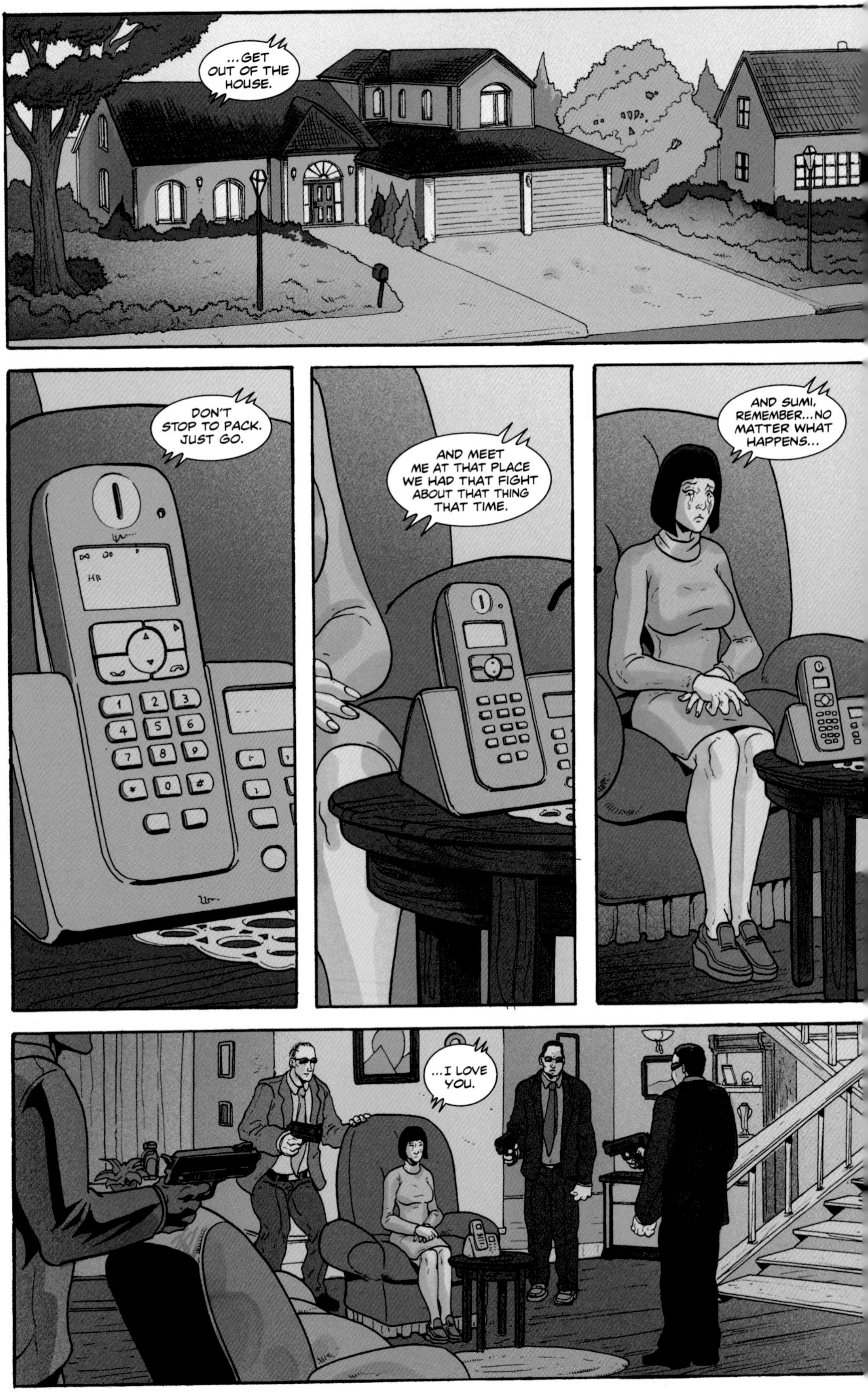
...GET OUT OF THE HOUSE.
DON'T STOP TO PACK. JUST GO.
AND MEET ME AT THAT PLACE WE HAD THAT FIGHT ABOUT THAT THING THAT TIME.
AND SUMI, REMEMBER...NO MATTER WHAT HAPPENS...
...I LOVE YOU.

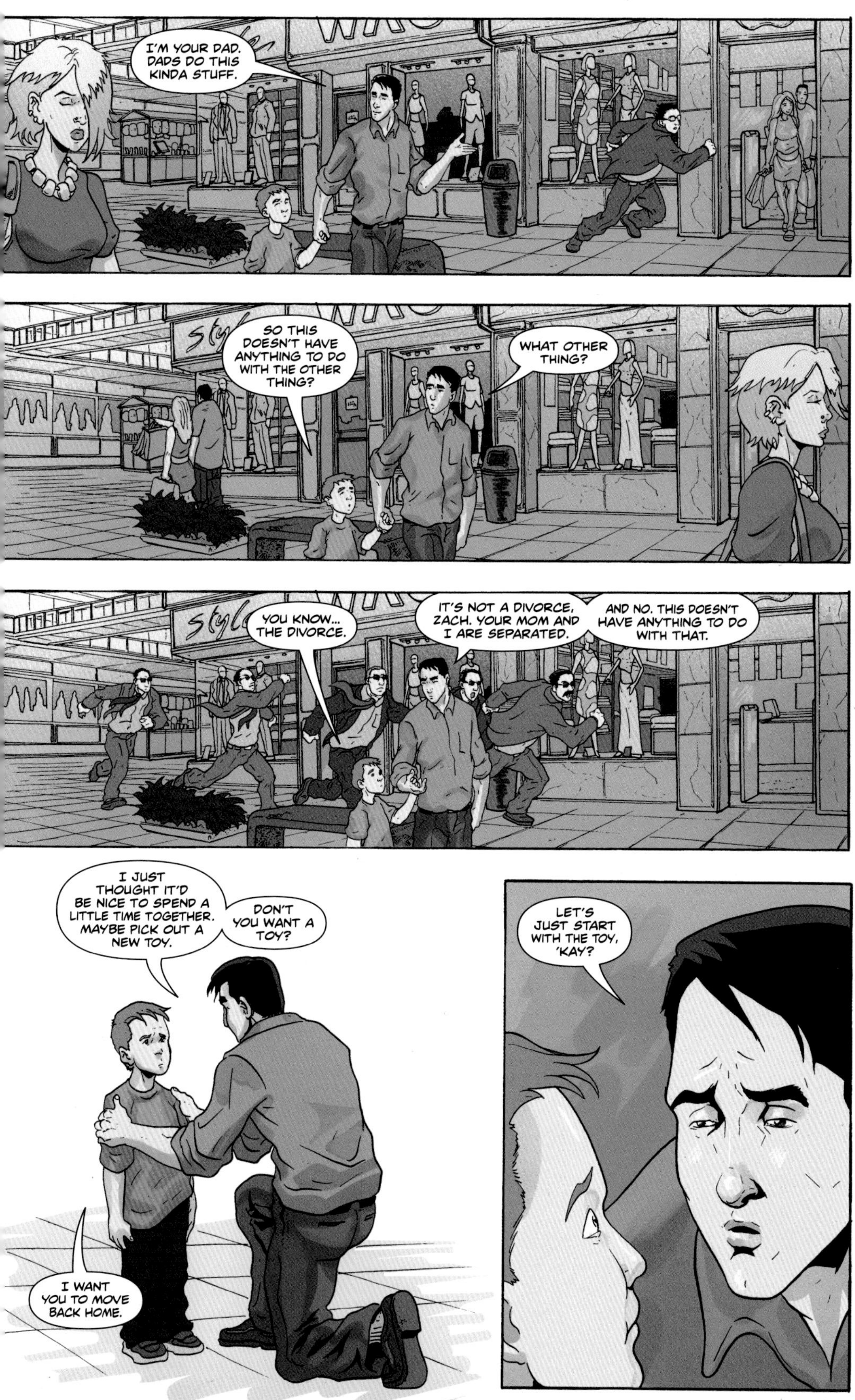
I'M YOUR DAD. DADS DO THIS KINDA STUFF.
SO THIS DOESN'T HAVE ANYTHING TO DO WITH THE OTHER THING?
WHAT OTHER THING?
YOU KNOW... THE DIVORCE.
IT'S NOT A DIVORCE, ZACH. YOUR MOM AND I ARE SEPARATED.
AND NO. THIS DOESN'T HAVE ANYTHING TO DO WITH THAT.
I JUST THOUGHT IT'D BE NICE TO SPEND A LITTLE TIME TOGETHER. MAYBE PICK OUT A NEW TOY.
DON'T YOU WANT A TOY?
I WANT YOU TO MOVE BACK HOME.
LET'S JUST START WITH THE TOY, 'KAY?

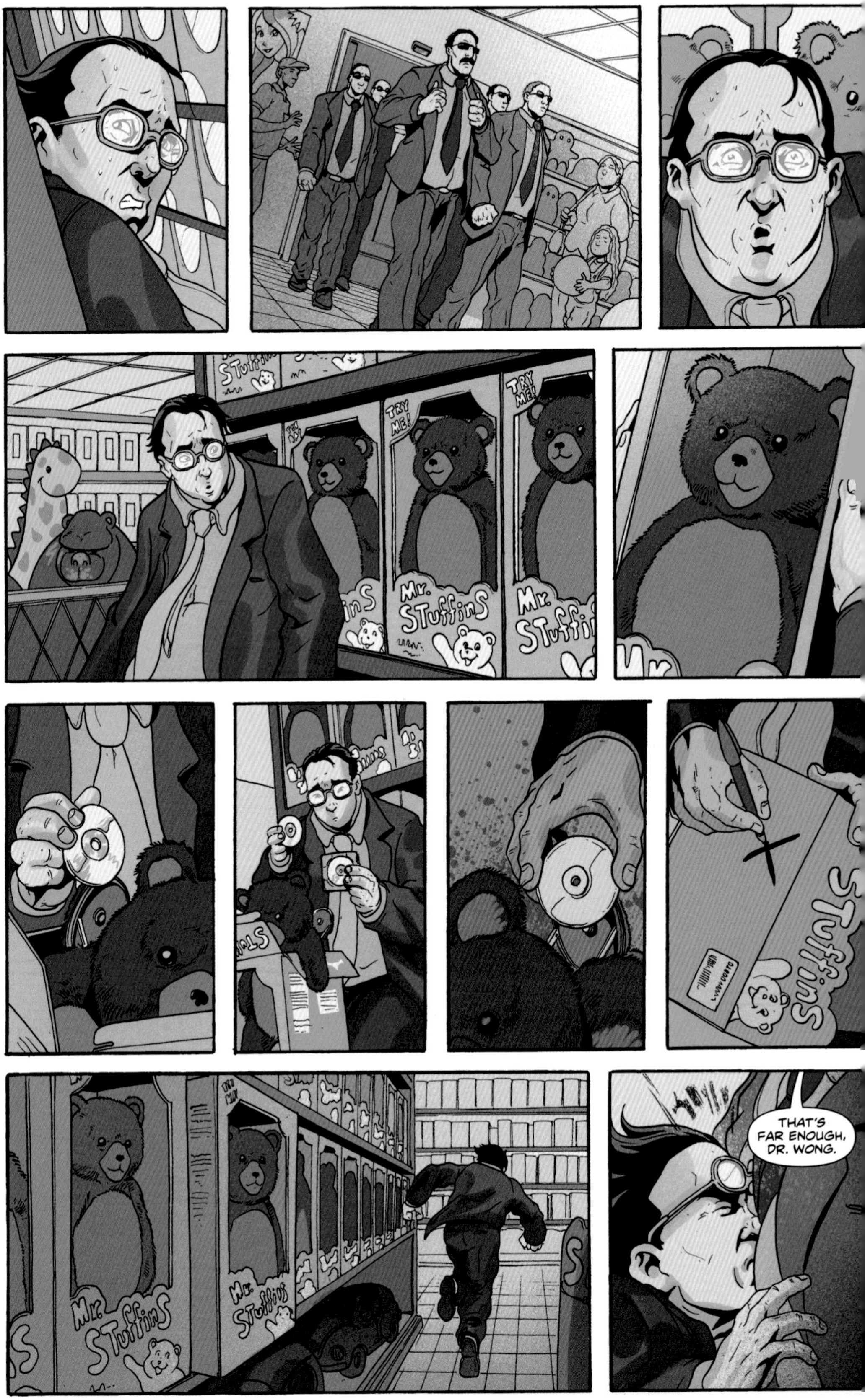
TRY ME!
TRY ME!
Mr. Stuffins
Mr. Stuffins
Stuffins
Mr. Stuffins
Mr. Stuffins
THAT'S FAR ENOUGH, DR. WONG.

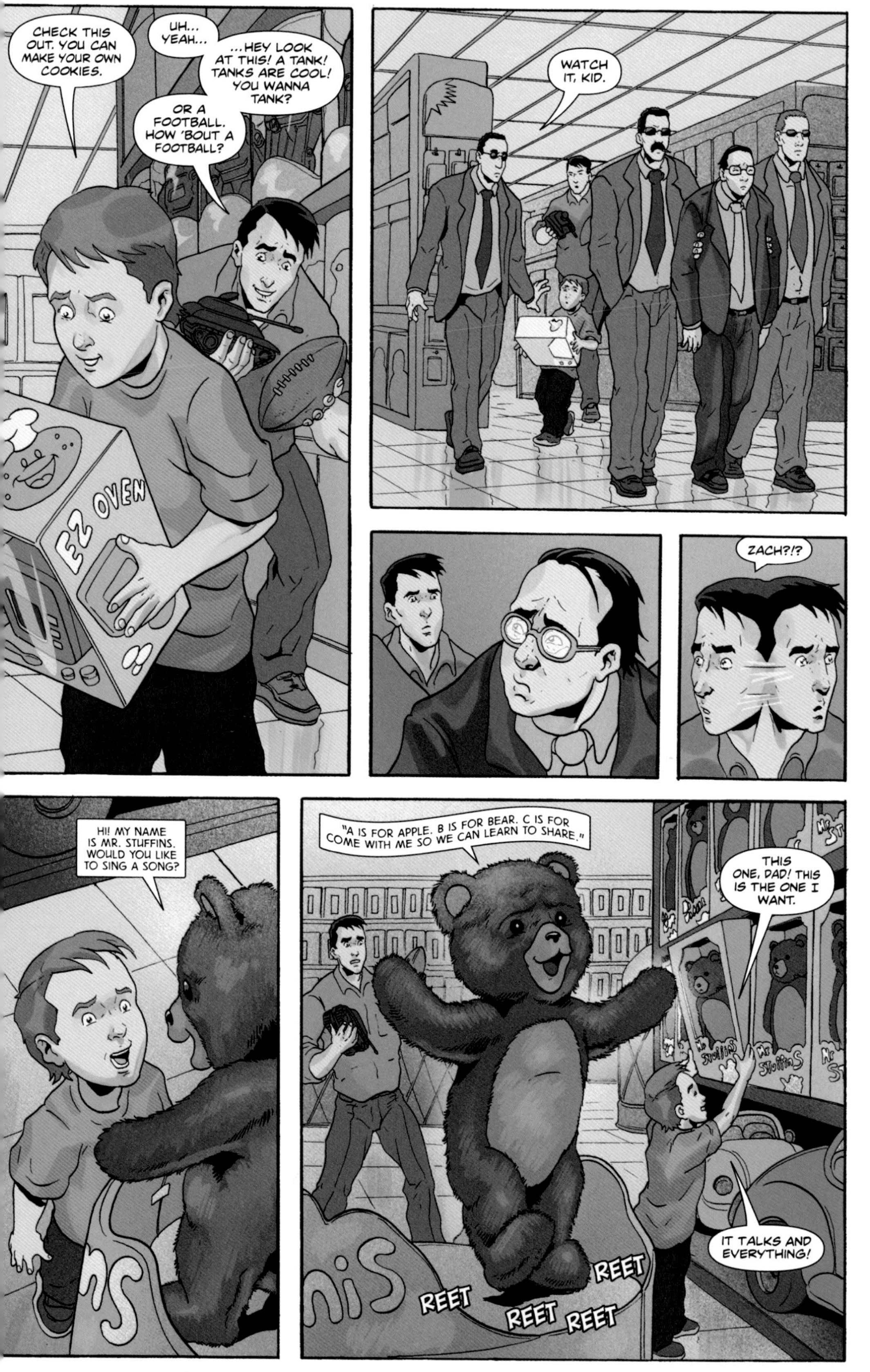
CHECK THIS OUT. YOU CAN MAKE YOUR OWN COOKIES.
UH... YEAH...
...HEY LOOK AT THIS! A TANK! TANKS ARE COOL! YOU WANNA TANK?
OR A FOOTBALL. HOW 'BOUT A FOOTBALL?
EZ OVEN
WATCH IT, KID.
ZACH?!?
HI! MY NAME IS MR. STUFFINS. WOULD YOU LIKE TO SING A SONG?
"A IS FOR APPLE. B IS FOR BEAR. C IS FOR COME WITH ME SO WE CAN LEARN TO SHARE."
THIS ONE, DAD! THIS IS THE ONE I WANT.
IT TALKS AND EVERYTHING!
REET
REET
REET
REET

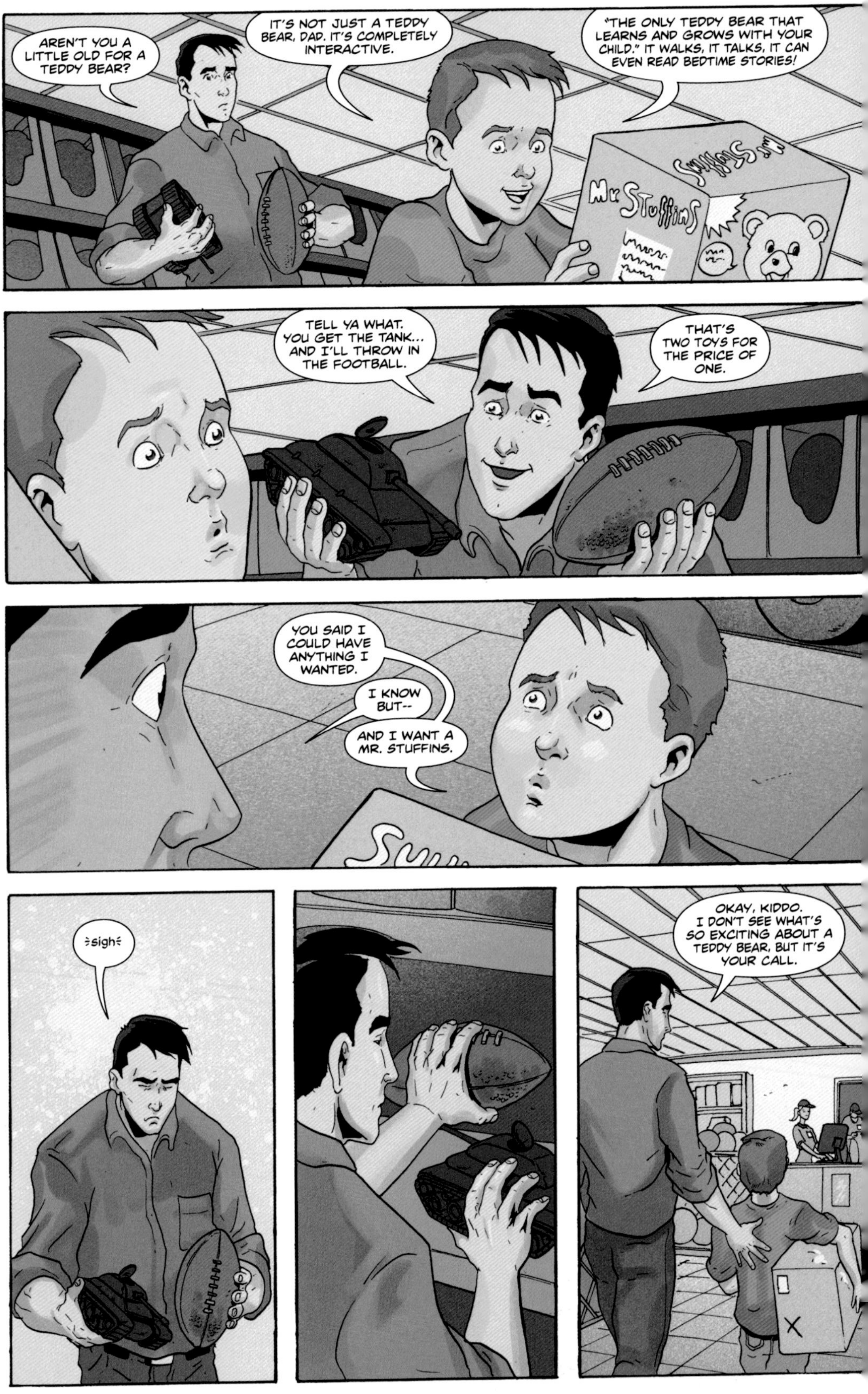
AREN'T YOU A LITTLE OLD FOR A TEDDY BEAR?
IT'S NOT JUST A TEDDY BEAR, DAD. IT'S COMPLETELY INTERACTIVE.
"THE ONLY TEDDY BEAR THAT LEARNS AND GROWS WITH YOUR CHILD." IT WALKS, IT TALKS, IT CAN EVEN READ BEDTIME STORIES!
MR STUFFINS
TELL YA WHAT. YOU GET THE TANK... AND I'LL THROW IN THE FOOTBALL.
THAT'S TWO TOYS FOR THE PRICE OF ONE.
YOU SAID I COULD HAVE ANYTHING I WANTED.
I KNOW BUT--
AND I WANT A MR. STUFFINS.
sigh
OKAY, KIDDO. I DON'T SEE WHAT'S SO EXCITING ABOUT A TEDDY BEAR, BUT IT'S YOUR CALL.

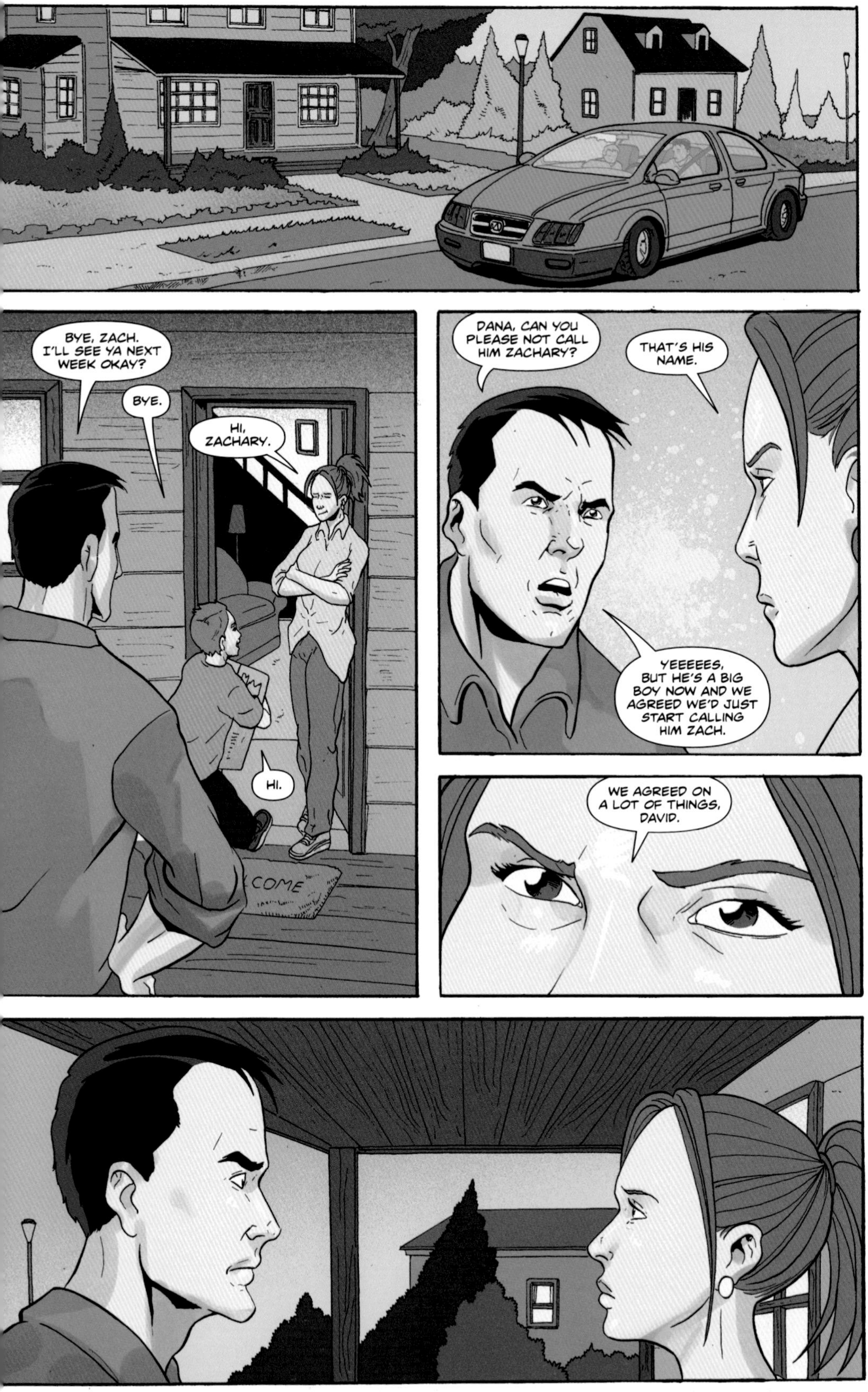
BYE, ZACH. I'LL SEE YA NEXT WEEK OKAY?
BYE.
HI, ZACHARY.
HI.
DANA, CAN YOU PLEASE NOT CALL HIM ZACHARY?
THAT'S HIS NAME.
YEEEEES, BUT HE'S A BIG BOY NOW AND WE AGREED WE'D JUST START CALLING HIM ZACH.
WE AGREED ON A LOT OF THINGS, DAVID.

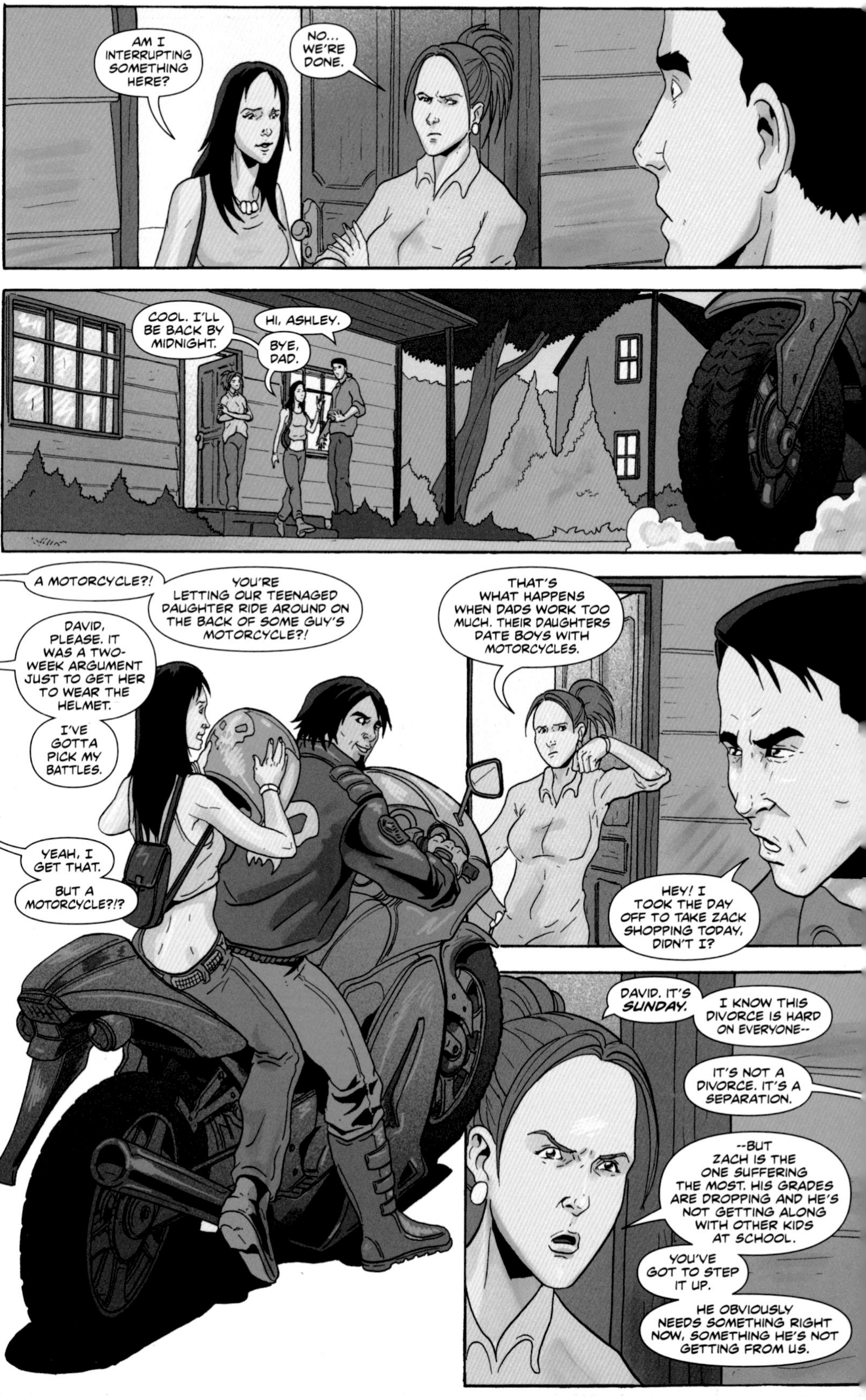
AM I INTERRUPTING SOMETHING HERE?
NO... WE'RE DONE.
COOL. I'LL BE BACK BY MIDNIGHT.
HI, ASHLEY.
BYE, DAD.
A MOTORCYCLE?!
YOU'RE LETTING OUR TEENAGED DAUGHTER RIDE AROUND ON THE BACK OF SOME GUY'S MOTORCYCLE?!
DAVID, PLEASE. IT WAS A TWO-WEEK ARGUMENT JUST TO GET HER TO WEAR THE HELMET.
I'VE GOTTA PICK MY BATTLES.
YEAH, I GET THAT.
BUT A MOTORCYCLE?!?
THAT'S WHAT HAPPENS WHEN DADS WORK TOO MUCH. THEIR DAUGHTERS DATE BOYS WITH MOTORCYCLES.
HEY! I TOOK THE DAY OFF TO TAKE ZACK SHOPPING TODAY, DIDN'T I?
DAVID. IT'S **SUNDAY.**
I KNOW THIS DIVORCE IS HARD ON EVERYONE--
IT'S NOT A DIVORCE. IT'S A SEPARATION.
--BUT ZACH IS THE ONE SUFFERING THE MOST. HIS GRADES ARE DROPPING AND HE'S NOT GETTING ALONG WITH OTHER KIDS AT SCHOOL.
YOU'VE GOT TO STEP IT UP.
HE OBVIOUSLY NEEDS SOMETHING RIGHT NOW, SOMETHING HE'S NOT GETTING FROM US.

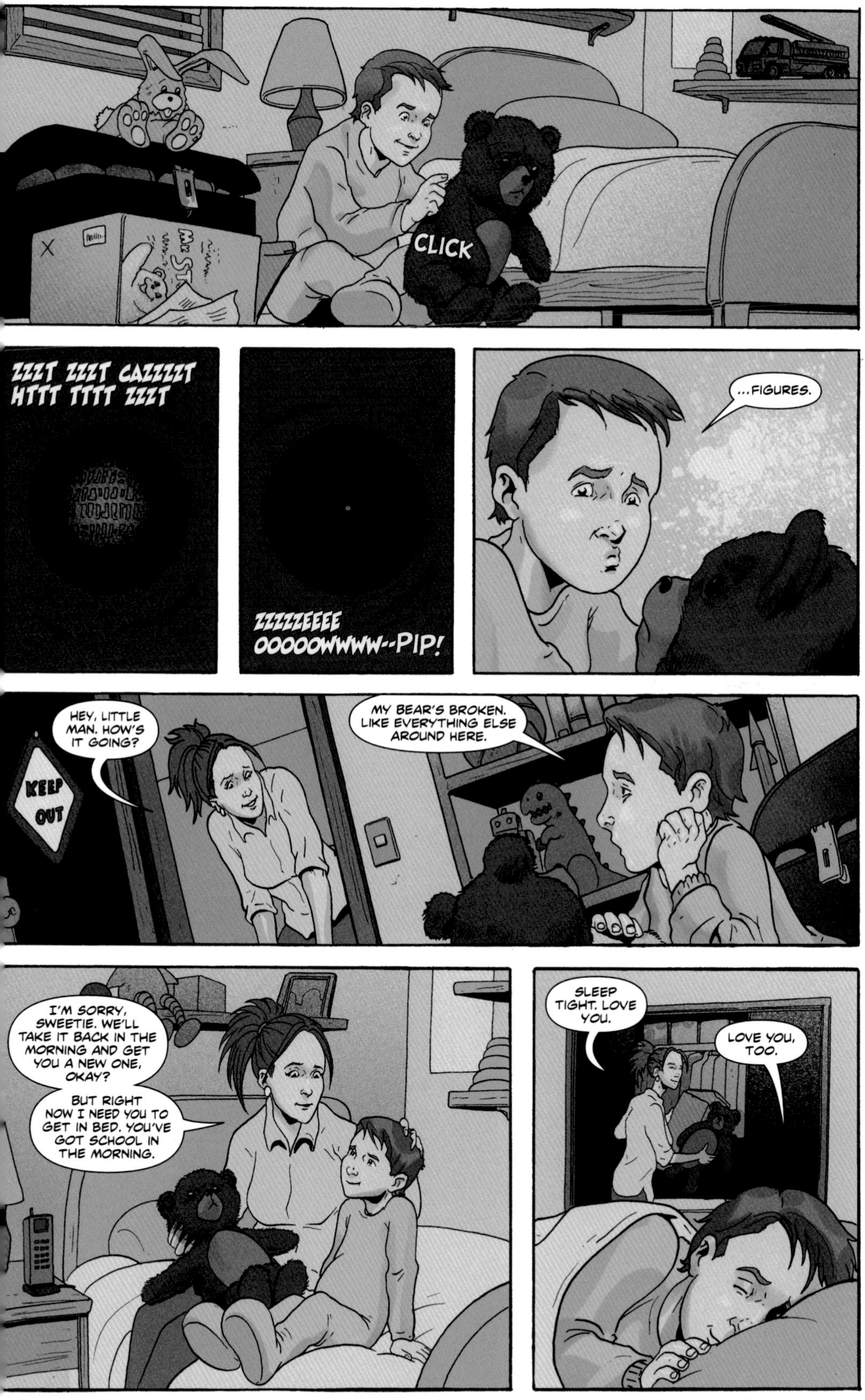

Mr. ST
CLICK
ZZZT ZZZT CAZZZZT HTTT TTTT ZZZT
ZZZZZEEEE OOOOOWWWW--PIP!
...FIGURES.
HEY, LITTLE MAN. HOW'S IT GOING?
KEEP OUT
MY BEAR'S BROKEN. LIKE EVERYTHING ELSE AROUND HERE.
I'M SORRY, SWEETIE. WE'LL TAKE IT BACK IN THE MORNING AND GET YOU A NEW ONE, OKAY?
BUT RIGHT NOW I NEED YOU TO GET IN BED. YOU'VE GOT SCHOOL IN THE MORNING.
SLEEP TIGHT. LOVE YOU.
LOVE YOU, TOO.

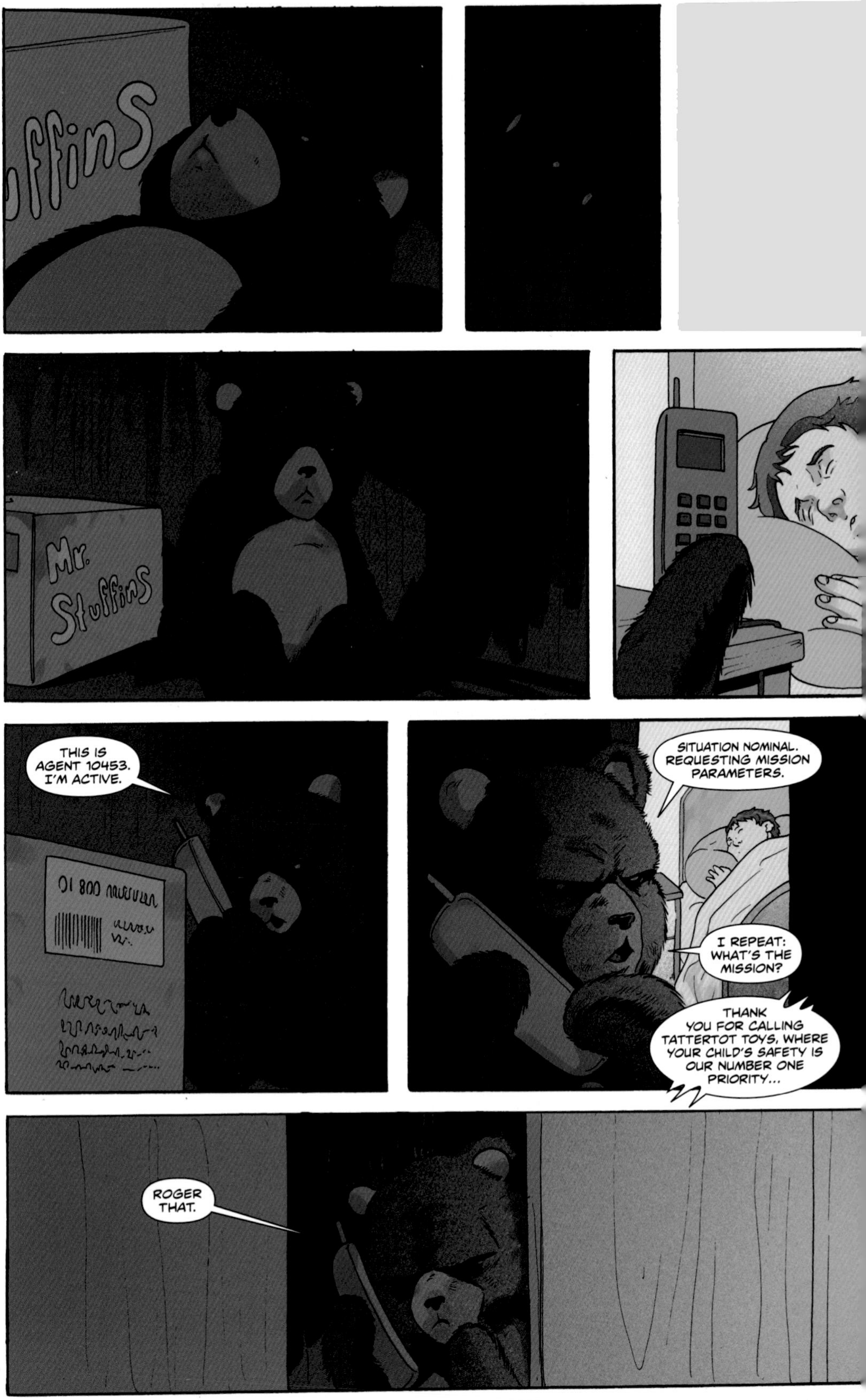
Mr. Stuffins
THIS IS AGENT 10453. I'M ACTIVE.
SITUATION NOMINAL. REQUESTING MISSION PARAMETERS.
I REPEAT: WHAT'S THE MISSION?
THANK YOU FOR CALLING TATTERTOT TOYS, WHERE YOUR CHILD'S SAFETY IS OUR NUMBER ONE PRIORITY...
ROGER THAT.

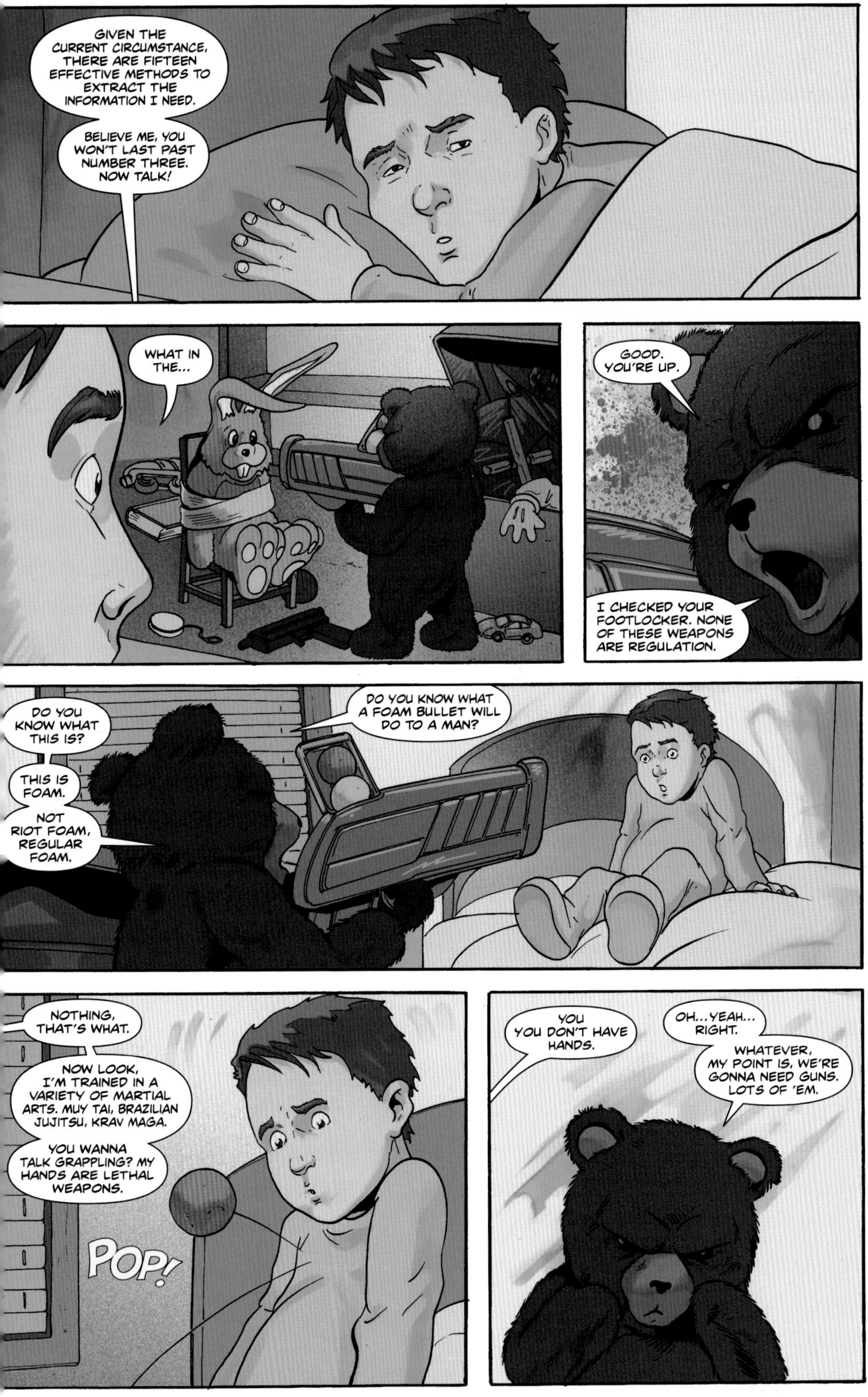
GIVEN THE CURRENT CIRCUMSTANCE, THERE ARE FIFTEEN EFFECTIVE METHODS TO EXTRACT THE INFORMATION I NEED.
BELIEVE ME, YOU WON'T LAST PAST NUMBER THREE. NOW TALK!
WHAT IN THE...
GOOD. YOU'RE UP.
I CHECKED YOUR FOOTLOCKER. NONE OF THESE WEAPONS ARE REGULATION.
DO YOU KNOW WHAT THIS IS?
THIS IS FOAM.
NOT RIOT FOAM, REGULAR FOAM.
DO YOU KNOW WHAT A FOAM BULLET WILL DO TO A MAN?
NOTHING, THAT'S WHAT.
NOW LOOK, I'M TRAINED IN A VARIETY OF MARTIAL ARTS. MUY TAI, BRAZILIAN JUJITSU, KRAV MAGA.
YOU WANNA TALK GRAPPLING? MY HANDS ARE LETHAL WEAPONS.
POP!
YOU YOU DON'T HAVE HANDS.
OH...YEAH... RIGHT.
WHATEVER, MY POINT IS, WE'RE GONNA NEED GUNS. LOTS OF 'EM.

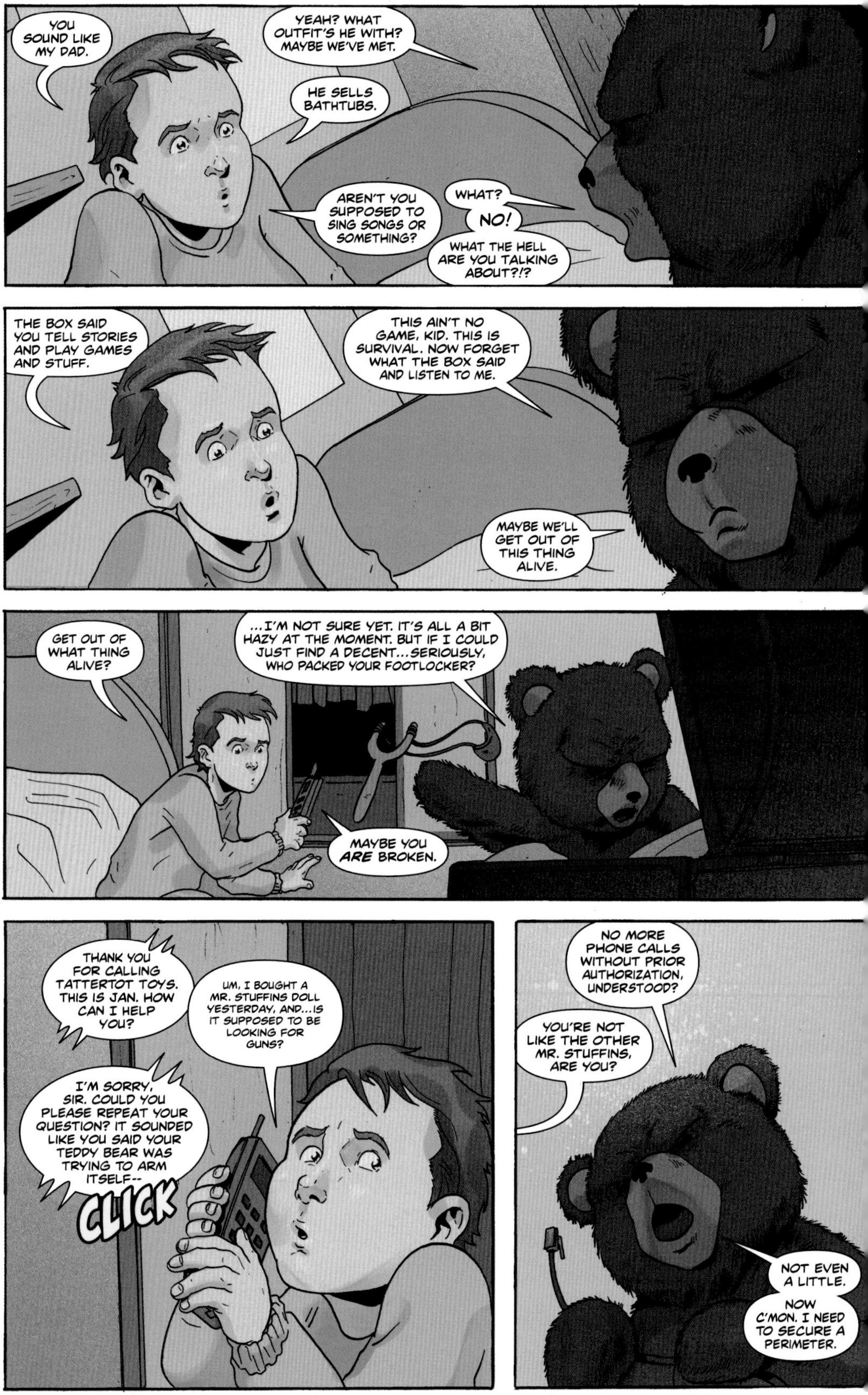
YOU SOUND LIKE MY DAD.
YEAH? WHAT OUTFIT'S HE WITH? MAYBE WE'VE MET.
HE SELLS BATHTUBS.
AREN'T YOU SUPPOSED TO SING SONGS OR SOMETHING?
WHAT?
NO!
WHAT THE HELL ARE YOU TALKING ABOUT?!?
THE BOX SAID YOU TELL STORIES AND PLAY GAMES AND STUFF.
THIS AIN'T NO GAME, KID. THIS IS SURVIVAL. NOW FORGET WHAT THE BOX SAID AND LISTEN TO ME.
MAYBE WE'LL GET OUT OF THIS THING ALIVE.
GET OUT OF WHAT THING ALIVE?
...I'M NOT SURE YET. IT'S ALL A BIT HAZY AT THE MOMENT. BUT IF I COULD JUST FIND A DECENT... SERIOUSLY, WHO PACKED YOUR FOOTLOCKER?
MAYBE YOU ARE BROKEN.
THANK YOU FOR CALLING TATTERTOT TOYS. THIS IS JAN. HOW CAN I HELP YOU?
UM, I BOUGHT A MR. STUFFINS DOLL YESTERDAY, AND... IS IT SUPPOSED TO BE LOOKING FOR GUNS?
I'M SORRY, SIR. COULD YOU PLEASE REPEAT YOUR QUESTION? IT SOUNDED LIKE YOU SAID YOUR TEDDY BEAR WAS TRYING TO ARM ITSELF--
CLICK
NO MORE PHONE CALLS WITHOUT PRIOR AUTHORIZATION, UNDERSTOOD?
YOU'RE NOT LIKE THE OTHER MR. STUFFINS, ARE YOU?
NOT EVEN A LITTLE.
NOW C'MON. I NEED TO SECURE A PERIMETER.

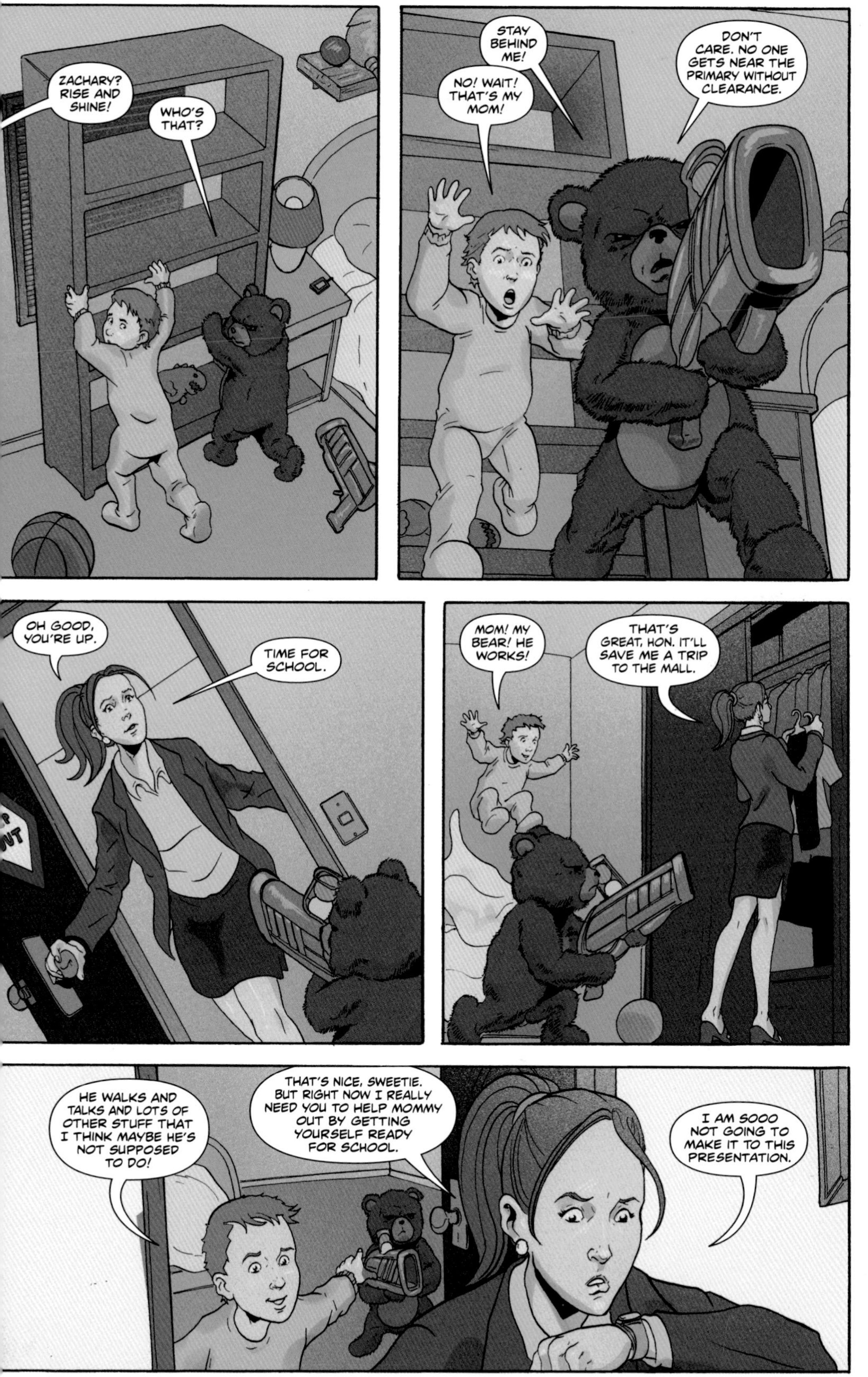
ZACHARY? RISE AND SHINE!
WHO'S THAT?
STAY BEHIND ME!
NO! WAIT! THAT'S MY MOM!
DON'T CARE. NO ONE GETS NEAR THE PRIMARY WITHOUT CLEARANCE.
OH GOOD, YOU'RE UP.
TIME FOR SCHOOL.
MOM! MY BEAR! HE WORKS!
THAT'S GREAT, HON. IT'LL SAVE ME A TRIP TO THE MALL.
HE WALKS AND TALKS AND LOTS OF OTHER STUFF THAT I THINK MAYBE HE'S NOT SUPPOSED TO DO!
THAT'S NICE, SWEETIE. BUT RIGHT NOW I REALLY NEED YOU TO HELP MOMMY OUT BY GETTING YOURSELF READY FOR SCHOOL.
I AM SOOO NOT GOING TO MAKE IT TO THIS PRESENTATION.

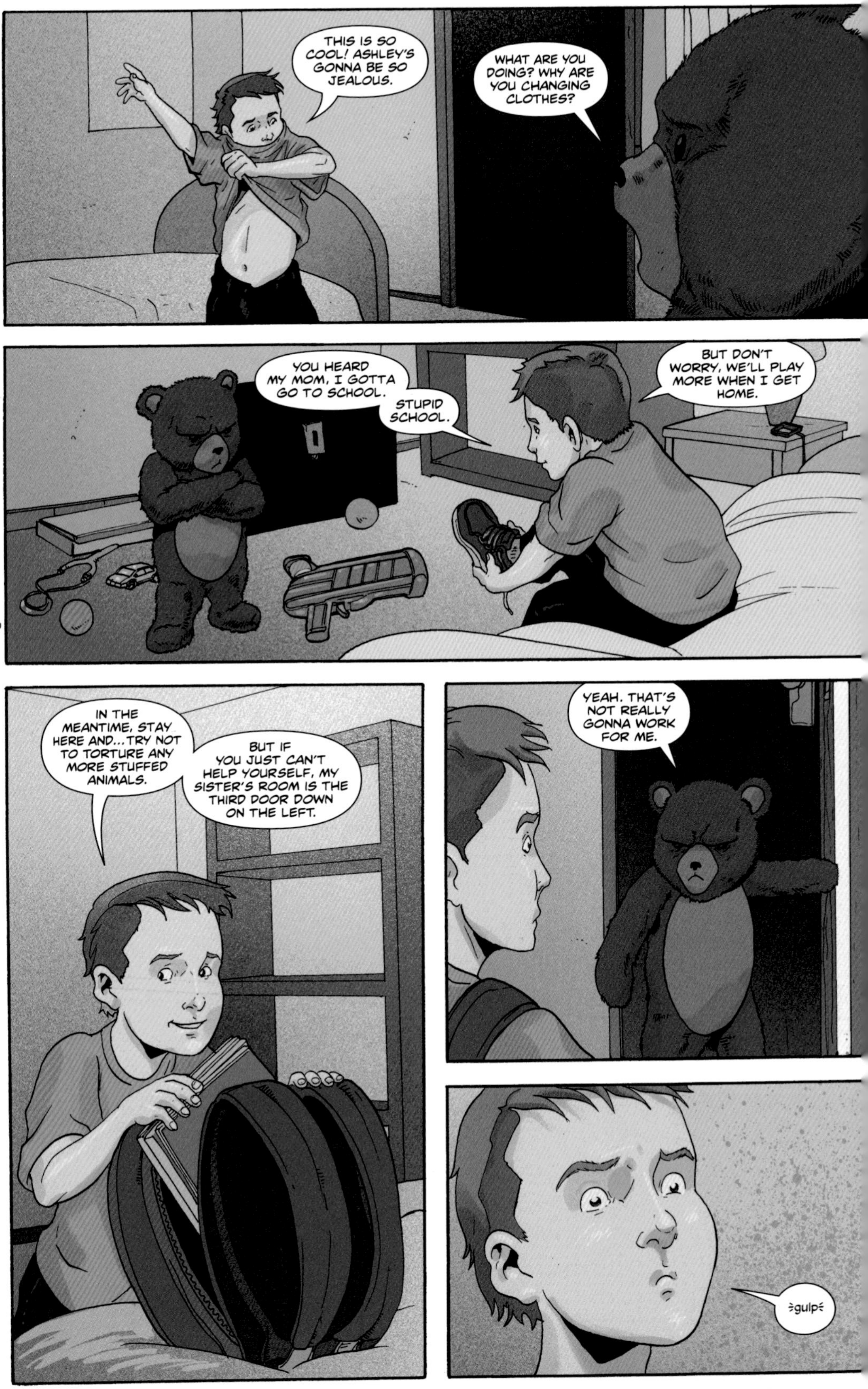
THIS IS SO COOL! ASHLEY'S GONNA BE SO JEALOUS.
WHAT ARE YOU DOING? WHY ARE YOU CHANGING CLOTHES?
YOU HEARD MY MOM, I GOTTA GO TO SCHOOL.
STUPID SCHOOL.
BUT DON'T WORRY, WE'LL PLAY MORE WHEN I GET HOME.
IN THE MEANTIME, STAY HERE AND...TRY NOT TO TORTURE ANY MORE STUFFED ANIMALS.
BUT IF YOU JUST CAN'T HELP YOURSELF, MY SISTER'S ROOM IS THE THIRD DOOR DOWN ON THE LEFT.
YEAH. THAT'S NOT REALLY GONNA WORK FOR ME.
gulp

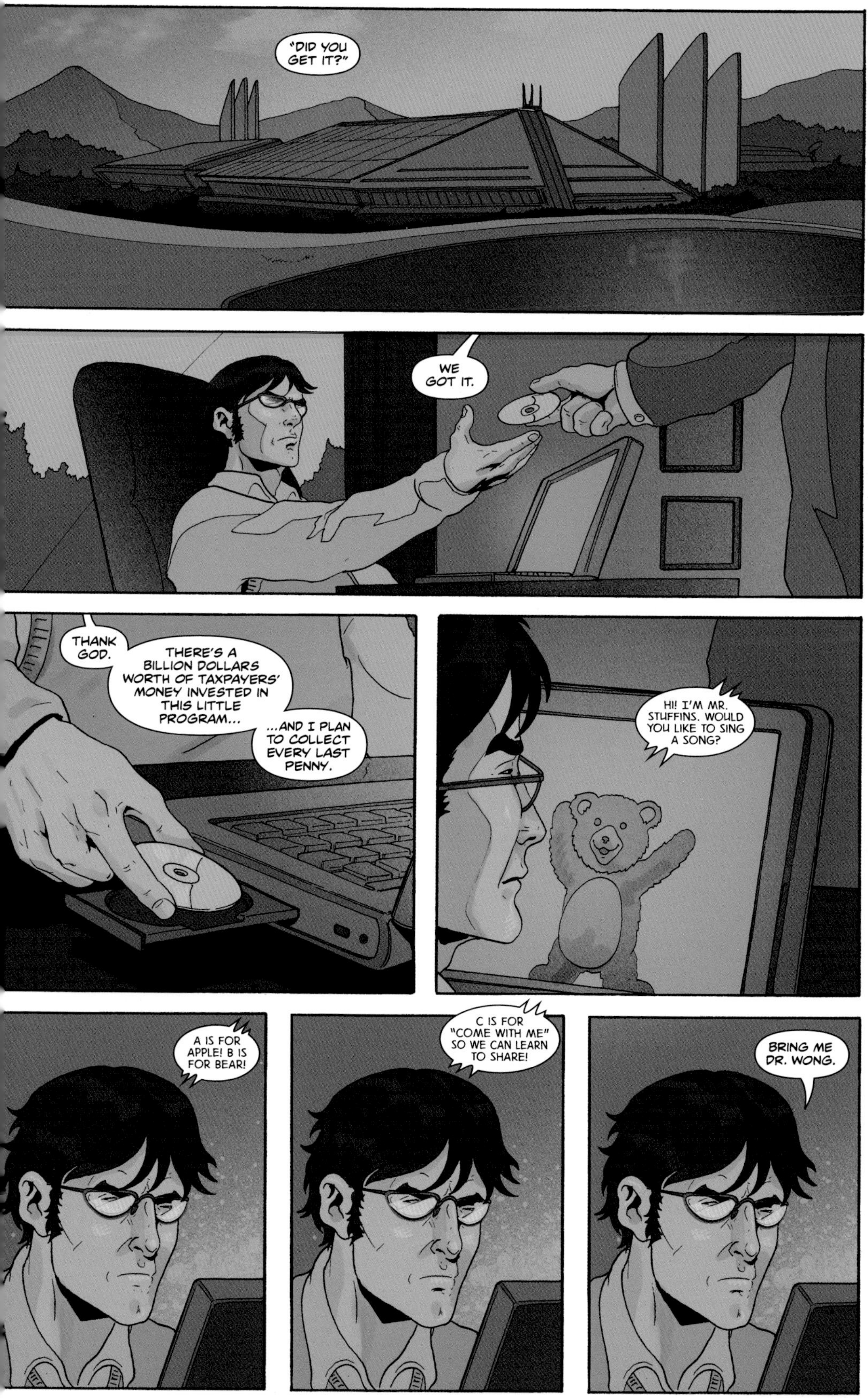
"DID YOU GET IT?"
WE GOT IT.
THANK GOD.
THERE'S A BILLION DOLLARS WORTH OF TAXPAYERS' MONEY INVESTED IN THIS LITTLE PROGRAM...
...AND I PLAN TO COLLECT EVERY LAST PENNY.
HI! I'M MR. STUFFINS. WOULD YOU LIKE TO SING A SONG?
A IS FOR APPLE! B IS FOR BEAR!
C IS FOR "COME WITH ME" SO WE CAN LEARN TO SHARE!
BRING ME DR. WONG.

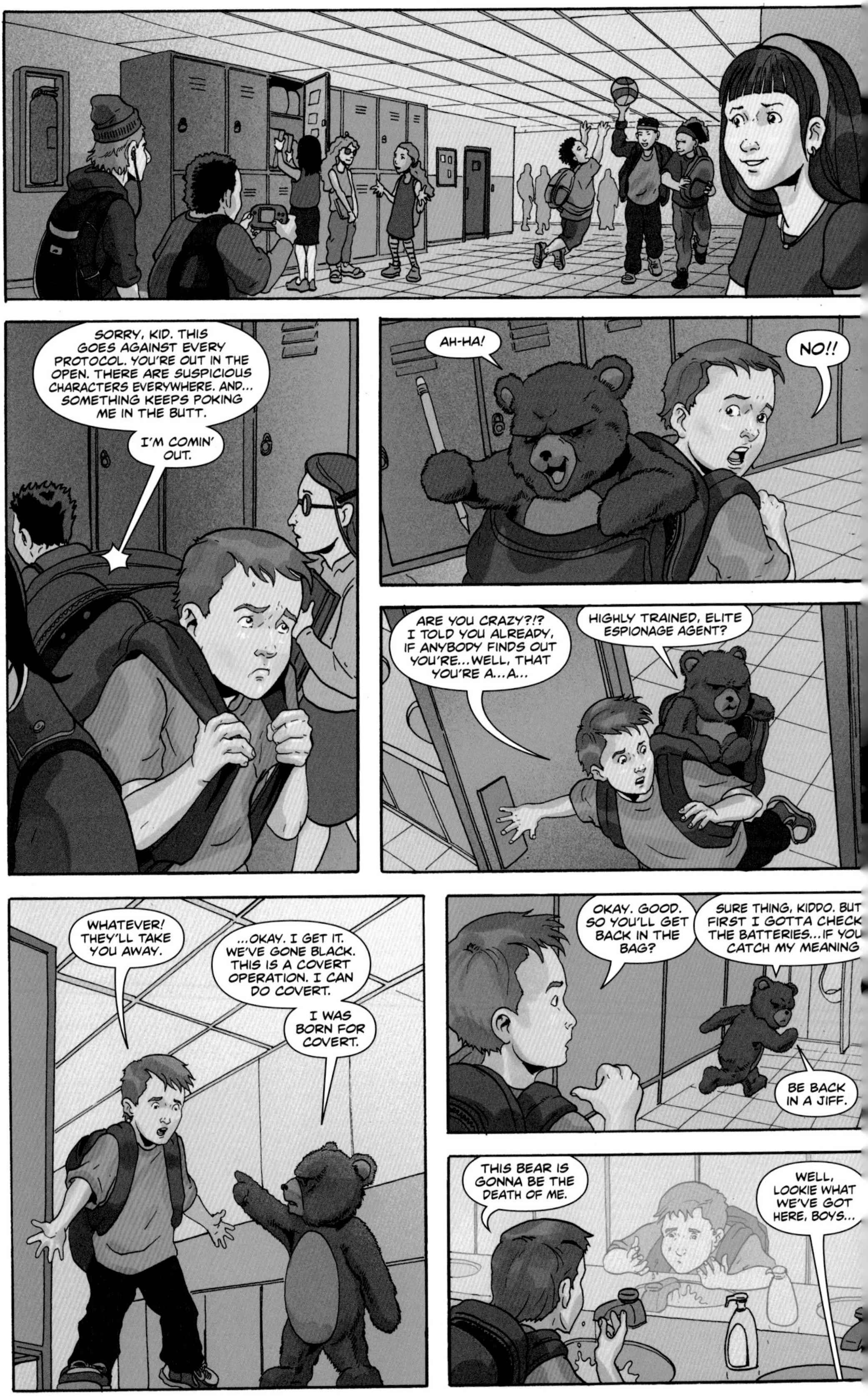
SORRY, KID. THIS GOES AGAINST EVERY PROTOCOL. YOU'RE OUT IN THE OPEN. THERE ARE SUSPICIOUS CHARACTERS EVERYWHERE. AND... SOMETHING KEEPS POKING ME IN THE BUTT.
I'M COMIN' OUT.
AH-HA!
NO!!
ARE YOU CRAZY?!? I TOLD YOU ALREADY, IF ANYBODY FINDS OUT YOU'RE...WELL, THAT YOU'RE A...A...
HIGHLY TRAINED, ELITE ESPIONAGE AGENT?
WHATEVER! THEY'LL TAKE YOU AWAY.
...OKAY. I GET IT. WE'VE GONE BLACK. THIS IS A COVERT OPERATION. I CAN DO COVERT.
I WAS BORN FOR COVERT.
OKAY. GOOD. SO YOU'LL GET BACK IN THE BAG?
SURE THING, KIDDO. BUT FIRST I GOTTA CHECK THE BATTERIES...IF YOU CATCH MY MEANING.
BE BACK IN A JIFF.
THIS BEAR IS GONNA BE THE DEATH OF ME.
WELL, LOOKIE WHAT WE'VE GOT HERE, BOYS...

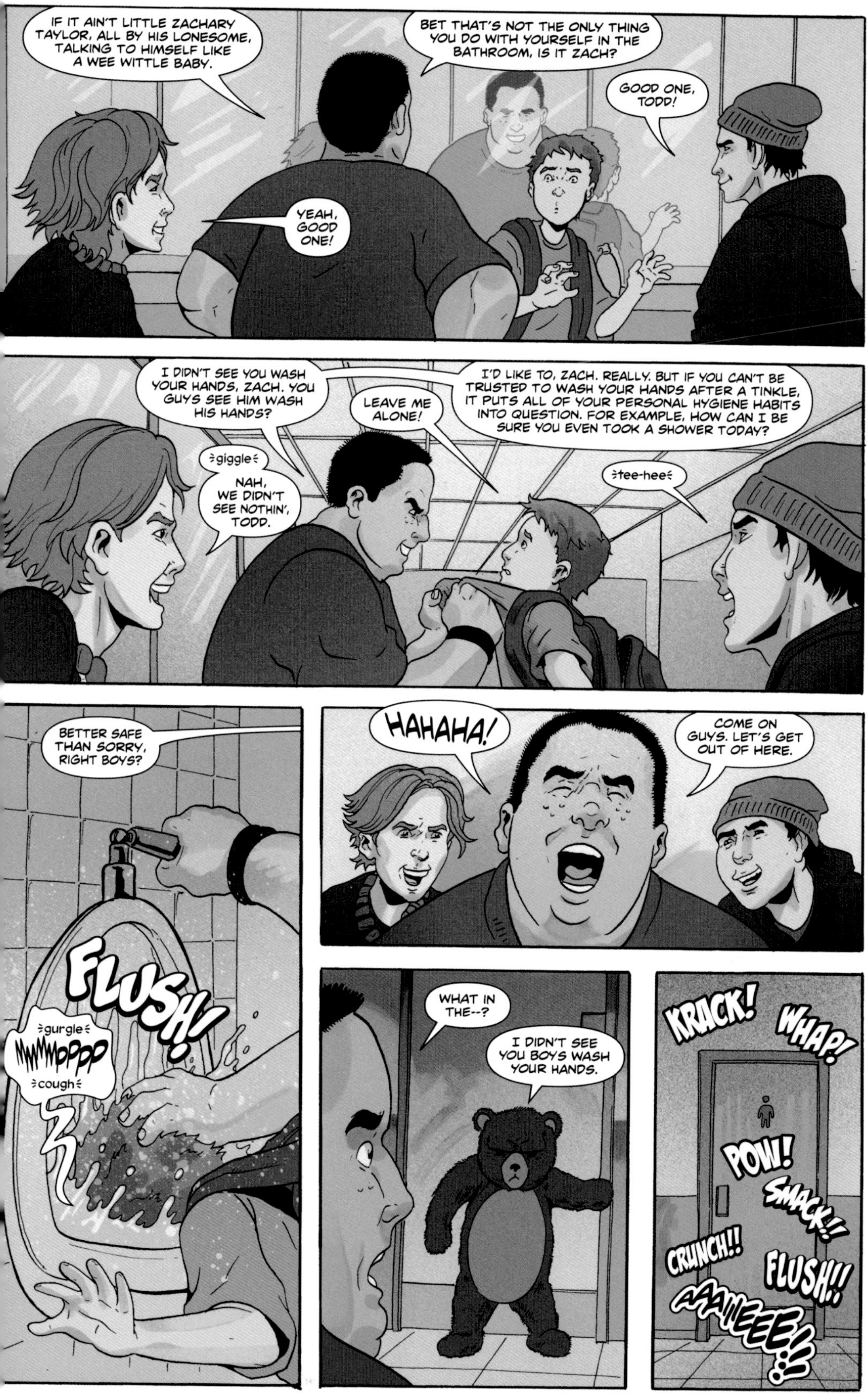
IF IT AIN'T LITTLE ZACHARY TAYLOR, ALL BY HIS LONESOME, TALKING TO HIMSELF LIKE A WEE WITTLE BABY.
BET THAT'S NOT THE ONLY THING YOU DO WITH YOURSELF IN THE BATHROOM, IS IT ZACH?
GOOD ONE, TODD!
YEAH, GOOD ONE!
I DIDN'T SEE YOU WASH YOUR HANDS, ZACH. YOU GUYS SEE HIM WASH HIS HANDS?
LEAVE ME ALONE!
I'D LIKE TO, ZACH. REALLY. BUT IF YOU CAN'T BE TRUSTED TO WASH YOUR HANDS AFTER A TINKLE, IT PUTS ALL OF YOUR PERSONAL HYGIENE HABITS INTO QUESTION. FOR EXAMPLE, HOW CAN I BE SURE YOU EVEN TOOK A SHOWER TODAY?
giggle
NAH, WE DIDN'T SEE NOTHIN', TODD.
tee-hee
BETTER SAFE THAN SORRY, RIGHT BOYS?
FLUSH!
gurgle
MMMMOPPP
cough
HAHAHA!
COME ON GUYS. LET'S GET OUT OF HERE.
WHAT IN THE--?
I DIDN'T SEE YOU BOYS WASH YOUR HANDS.
KRACK!
WHAP!
POW!
SMACK!!
CRUNCH!!
FLUSH!!
AAAWEEE!!!

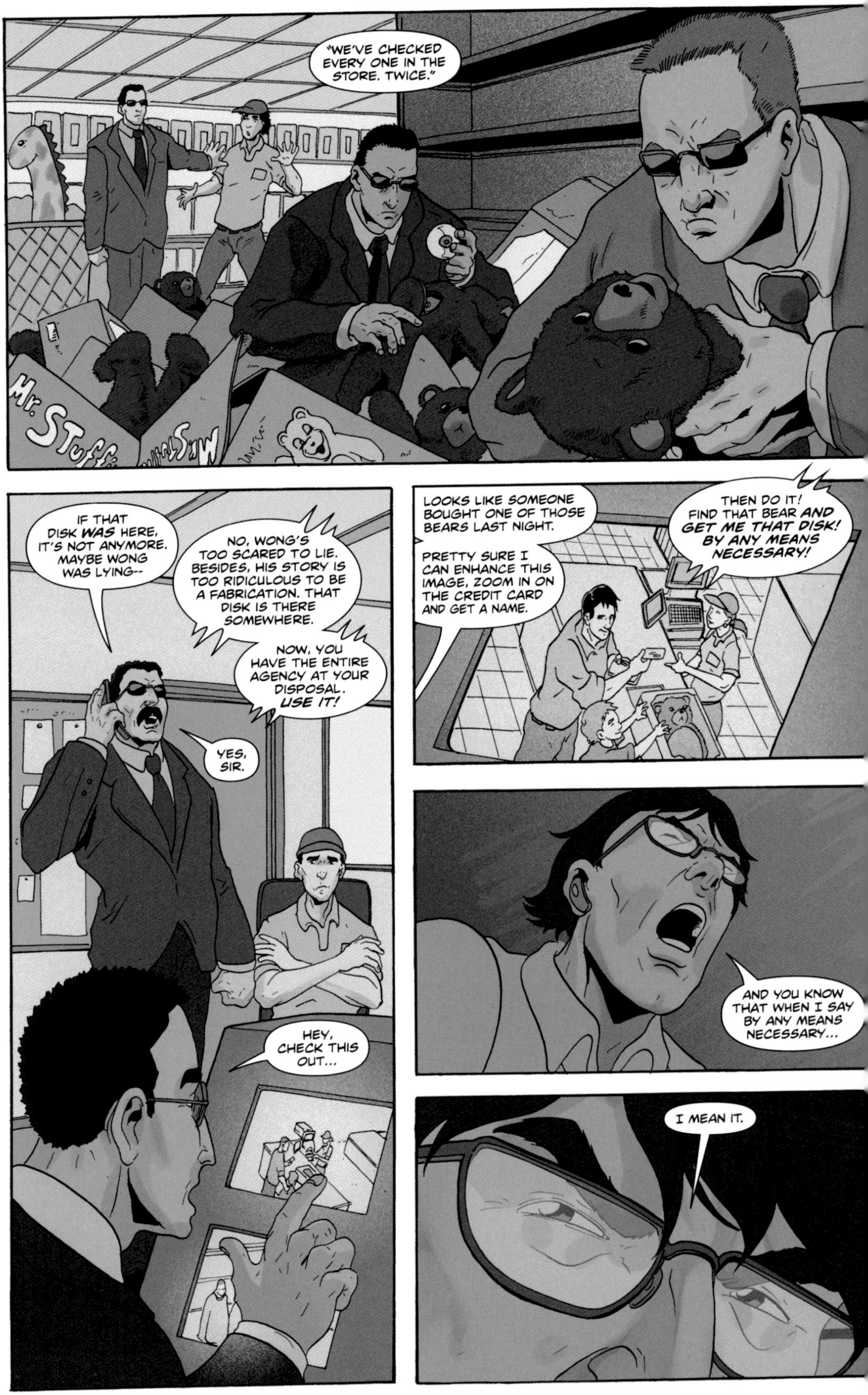

"WE'VE CHECKED EVERY ONE IN THE STORE. TWICE."
Mr. Stuffi
Mr. Stuffy
IF THAT DISK **WAS** HERE, IT'S NOT ANYMORE. MAYBE WONG WAS LYING--
NO, WONG'S TOO SCARED TO LIE. BESIDES, HIS STORY IS TOO RIDICULOUS TO BE A FABRICATION. THAT DISK IS THERE SOMEWHERE.
NOW, YOU HAVE THE ENTIRE AGENCY AT YOUR DISPOSAL. ***USE IT!***
YES, SIR.
HEY, CHECK THIS OUT...
LOOKS LIKE SOMEONE BOUGHT ONE OF THOSE BEARS LAST NIGHT.
PRETTY SURE I CAN ENHANCE THIS IMAGE, ZOOM IN ON THE CREDIT CARD AND GET A NAME.
THEN DO IT! FIND THAT BEAR ***AND GET ME THAT DISK! BY ANY MEANS NECESSARY!***
AND YOU KNOW THAT WHEN I SAY BY ANY MEANS NECESSARY...
I MEAN IT.

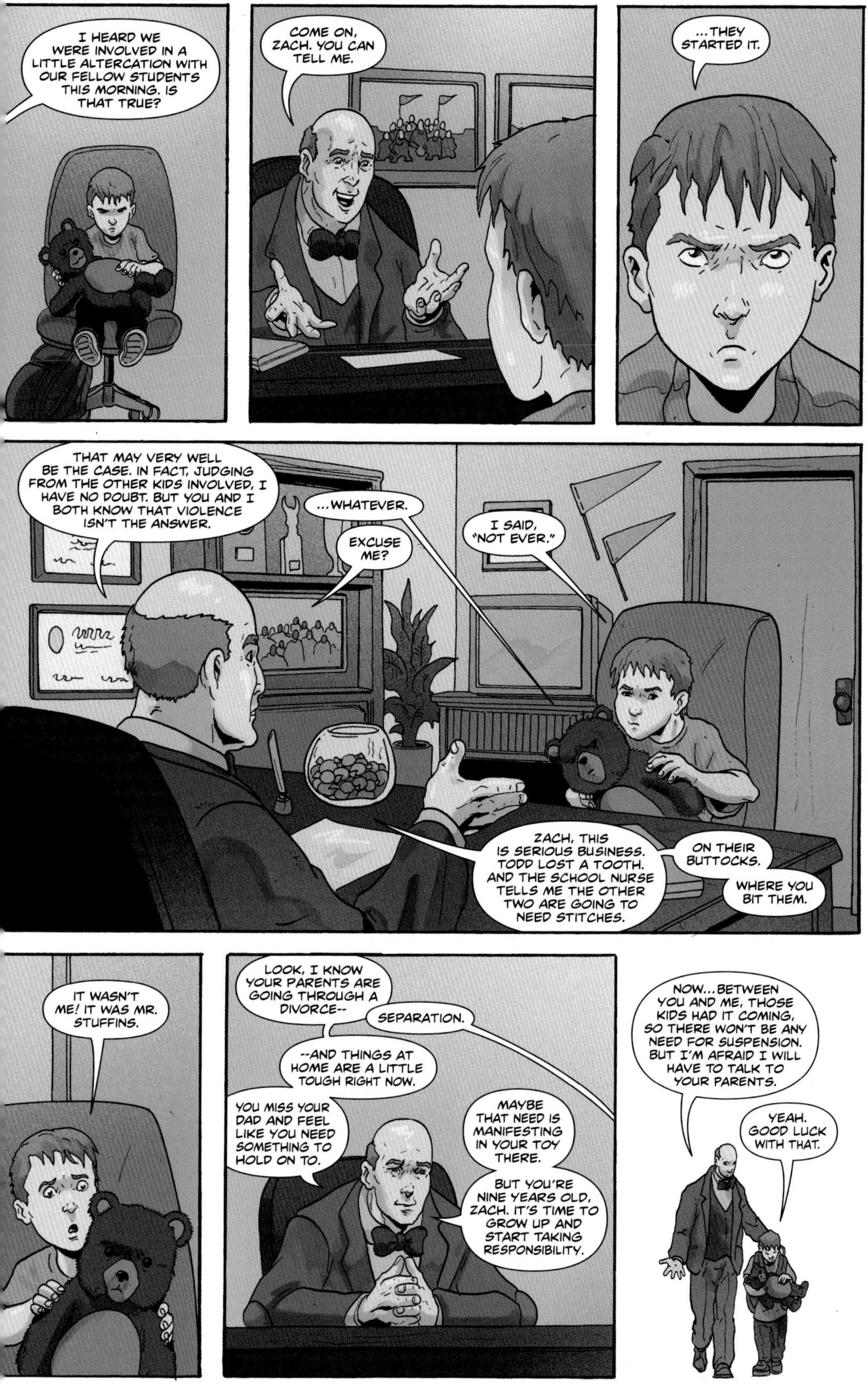
I HEARD WE WERE INVOLVED IN A LITTLE ALTERCATION WITH OUR FELLOW STUDENTS THIS MORNING. IS THAT TRUE?
COME ON, ZACH. YOU CAN TELL ME.
...THEY STARTED IT.
THAT MAY VERY WELL BE THE CASE. IN FACT, JUDGING FROM THE OTHER KIDS INVOLVED, I HAVE NO DOUBT. BUT YOU AND I BOTH KNOW THAT VIOLENCE ISN'T THE ANSWER.
...WHATEVER.
EXCUSE ME?
I SAID, "NOT EVER."
ZACH, THIS IS SERIOUS BUSINESS. TODD LOST A TOOTH. AND THE SCHOOL NURSE TELLS ME THE OTHER TWO ARE GOING TO NEED STITCHES.
ON THEIR BUTTOCKS.
WHERE YOU BIT THEM.
IT WASN'T ME! IT WAS MR. STUFFINS.
LOOK, I KNOW YOUR PARENTS ARE GOING THROUGH A DIVORCE--
SEPARATION.
--AND THINGS AT HOME ARE A LITTLE TOUGH RIGHT NOW.
YOU MISS YOUR DAD AND FEEL LIKE YOU NEED SOMETHING TO HOLD ON TO.
MAYBE THAT NEED IS MANIFESTING IN YOUR TOY THERE.
BUT YOU'RE NINE YEARS OLD, ZACH. IT'S TIME TO GROW UP AND START TAKING RESPONSIBILITY.
NOW...BETWEEN YOU AND ME, THOSE KIDS HAD IT COMING, SO THERE WON'T BE ANY NEED FOR SUSPENSION. BUT I'M AFRAID I WILL HAVE TO TALK TO YOUR PARENTS.
YEAH. GOOD LUCK WITH THAT.

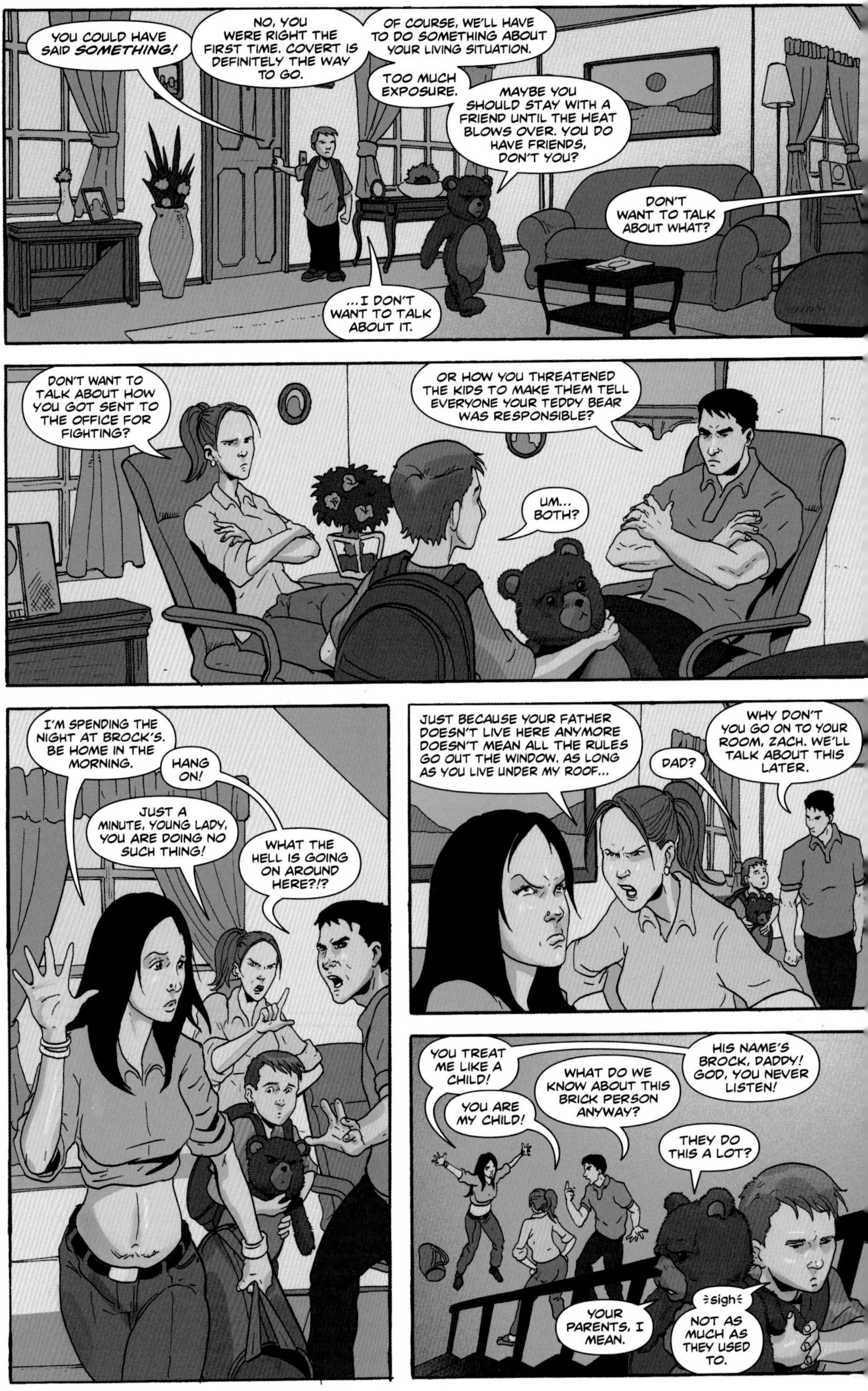
YOU COULD HAVE SAID SOMETHING!
NO, YOU WERE RIGHT THE FIRST TIME. COVERT IS DEFINITELY THE WAY TO GO.
OF COURSE, WE'LL HAVE TO DO SOMETHING ABOUT YOUR LIVING SITUATION.
TOO MUCH EXPOSURE.
MAYBE YOU SHOULD STAY WITH A FRIEND UNTIL THE HEAT BLOWS OVER. YOU DO HAVE FRIENDS, DON'T YOU?
...I DON'T WANT TO TALK ABOUT IT.
DON'T WANT TO TALK ABOUT WHAT?
DON'T WANT TO TALK ABOUT HOW YOU GOT SENT TO THE OFFICE FOR FIGHTING?
OR HOW YOU THREATENED THE KIDS TO MAKE THEM TELL EVERYONE YOUR TEDDY BEAR WAS RESPONSIBLE?
UM... BOTH?
I'M SPENDING THE NIGHT AT BROCK'S. BE HOME IN THE MORNING.
HANG ON!
JUST A MINUTE, YOUNG LADY, YOU ARE DOING NO SUCH THING!
WHAT THE HELL IS GOING ON AROUND HERE?!?
JUST BECAUSE YOUR FATHER DOESN'T LIVE HERE ANYMORE DOESN'T MEAN ALL THE RULES GO OUT THE WINDOW. AS LONG AS YOU LIVE UNDER MY ROOF...
DAD?
WHY DON'T YOU GO ON TO YOUR ROOM, ZACH. WE'LL TALK ABOUT THIS LATER.
YOU TREAT ME LIKE A CHILD!
YOU ARE MY CHILD!
WHAT DO WE KNOW ABOUT THIS BRICK PERSON ANYWAY?
HIS NAME'S BROCK, DADDY! GOD, YOU NEVER LISTEN!
THEY DO THIS A LOT?
YOUR PARENTS, I MEAN.
sigh
NOT AS MUCH AS THEY USED TO.

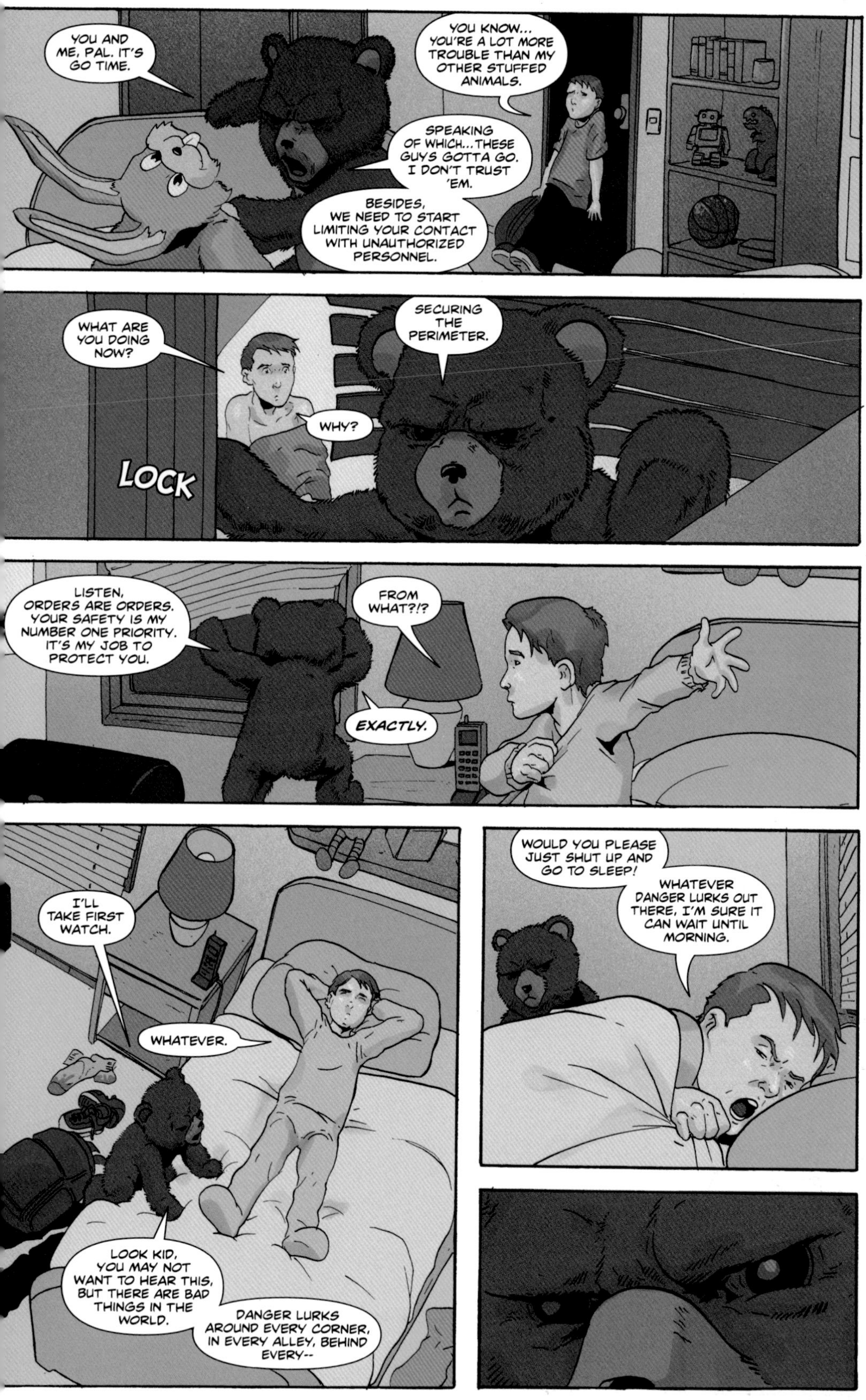

YOU AND ME, PAL. IT'S GO TIME.
YOU KNOW... YOU'RE A LOT MORE TROUBLE THAN MY OTHER STUFFED ANIMALS.
SPEAKING OF WHICH...THESE GUYS GOTTA GO. I DON'T TRUST 'EM.
BESIDES, WE NEED TO START LIMITING YOUR CONTACT WITH UNAUTHORIZED PERSONNEL.
WHAT ARE YOU DOING NOW?
SECURING THE PERIMETER.
WHY?
LOCK
LISTEN, ORDERS ARE ORDERS. YOUR SAFETY IS MY NUMBER ONE PRIORITY. IT'S MY JOB TO PROTECT YOU.
FROM WHAT?!?
EXACTLY.
I'LL TAKE FIRST WATCH.
WHATEVER.
LOOK KID, YOU MAY NOT WANT TO HEAR THIS, BUT THERE ARE BAD THINGS IN THE WORLD.
DANGER LURKS AROUND EVERY CORNER, IN EVERY ALLEY, BEHIND EVERY--
WOULD YOU PLEASE JUST SHUT UP AND GO TO SLEEP!
WHATEVER DANGER LURKS OUT THERE, I'M SURE IT CAN WAIT UNTIL MORNING.

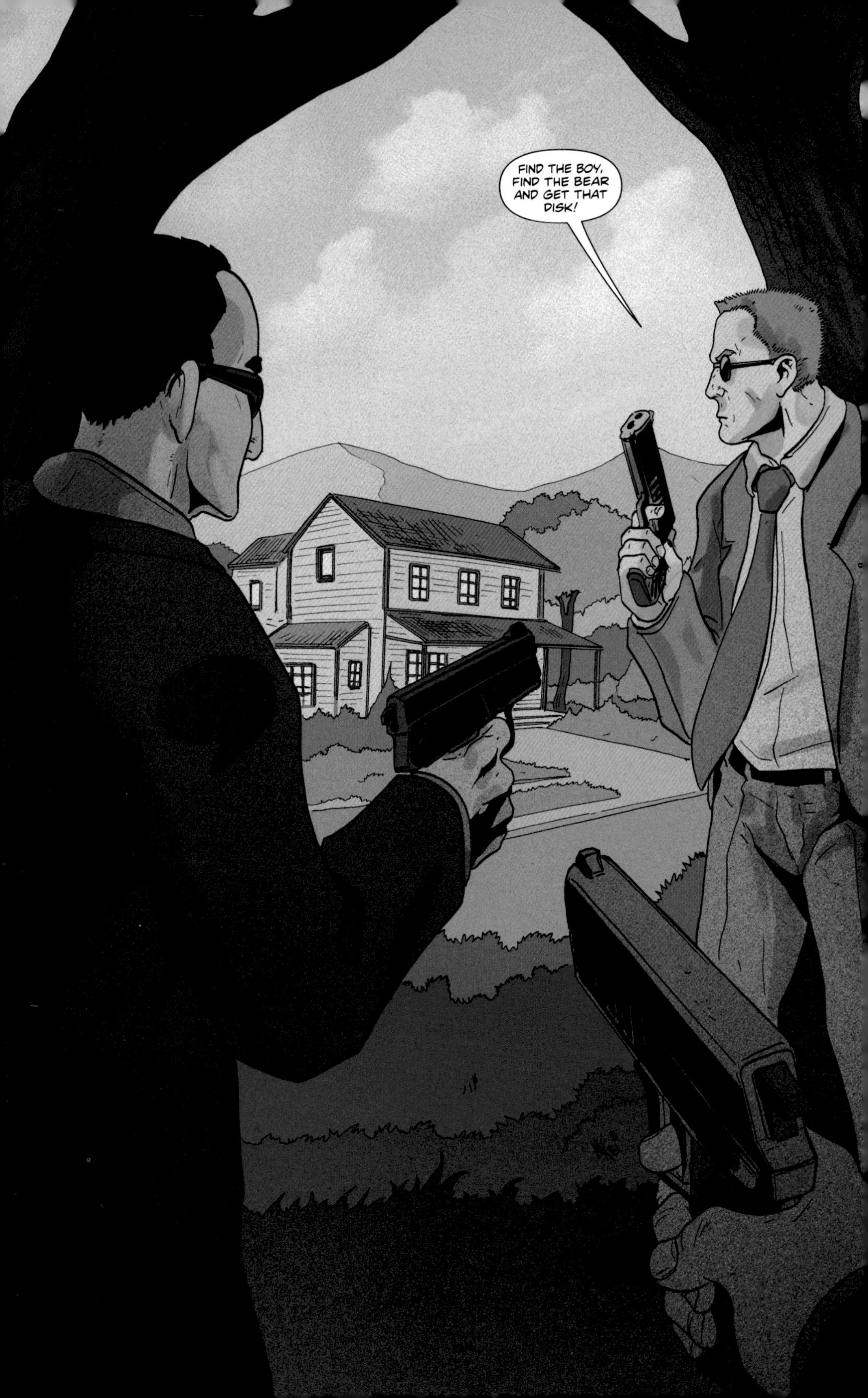
FIND THE BOY, FIND THE BEAR AND GET THAT DISK!

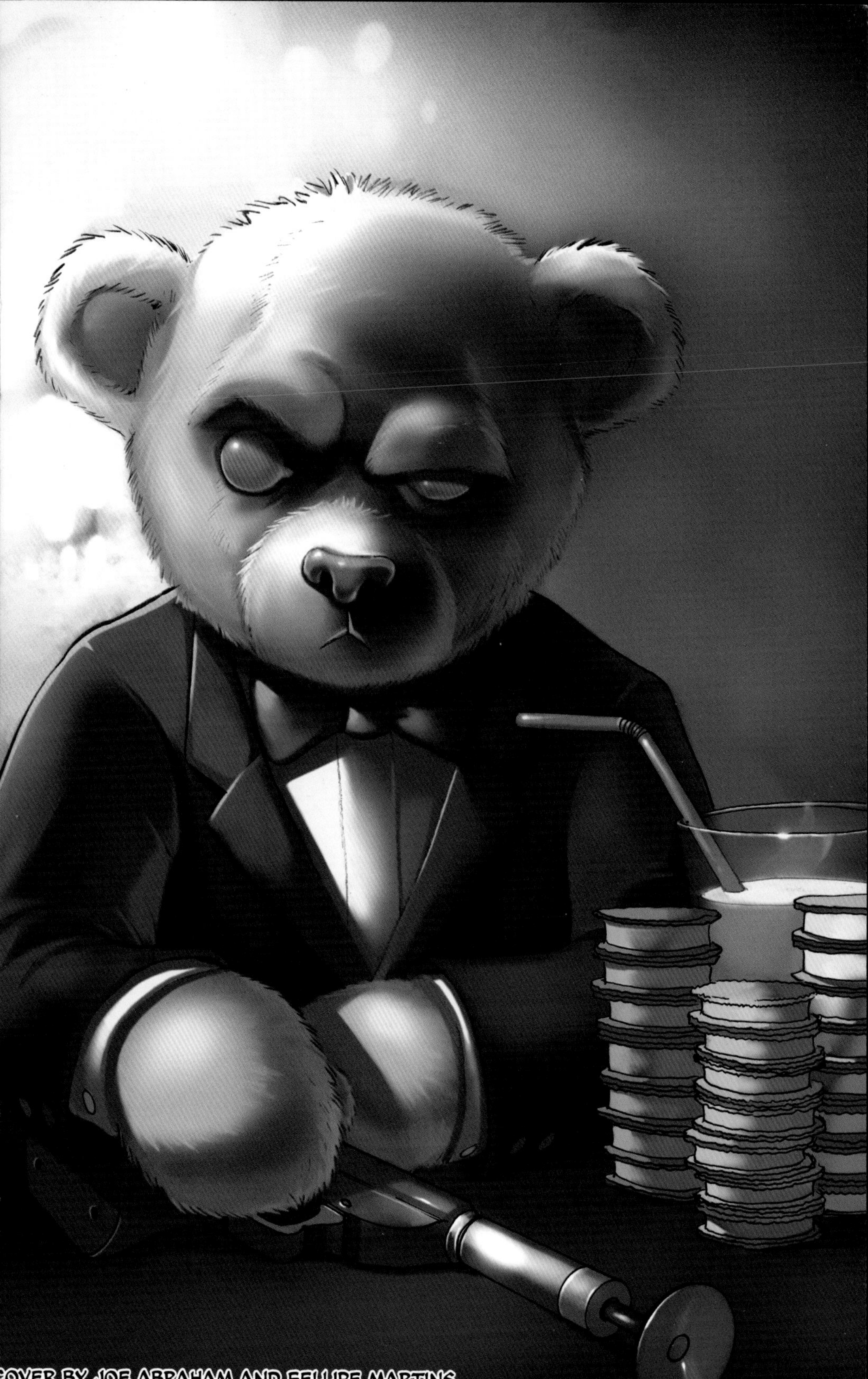

COVER BY JOE ABRAHAM AND FELLIPE MARTINS

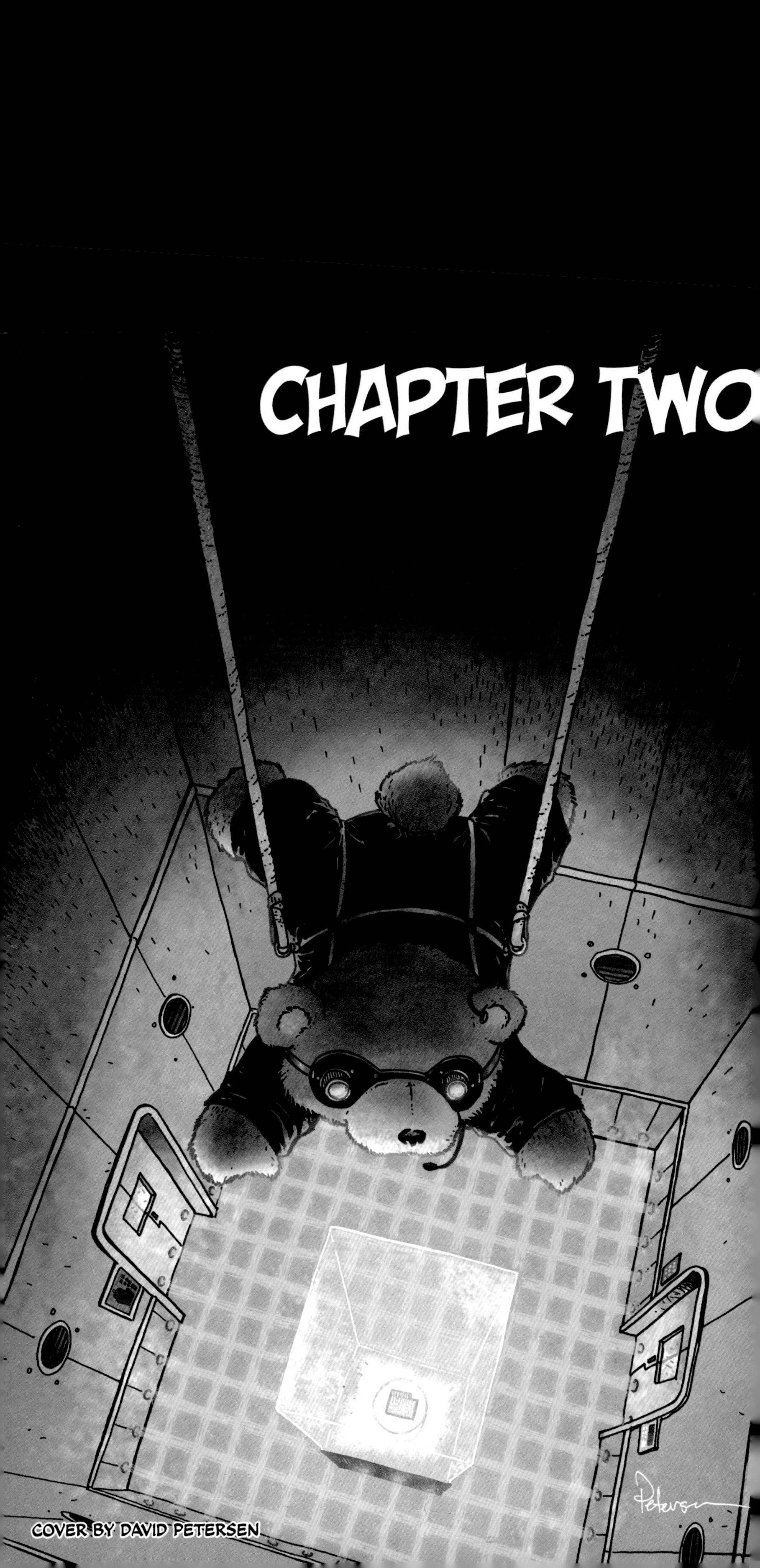
CHAPTER TWO
Petersen

COVER BY DAVID PETERSEN

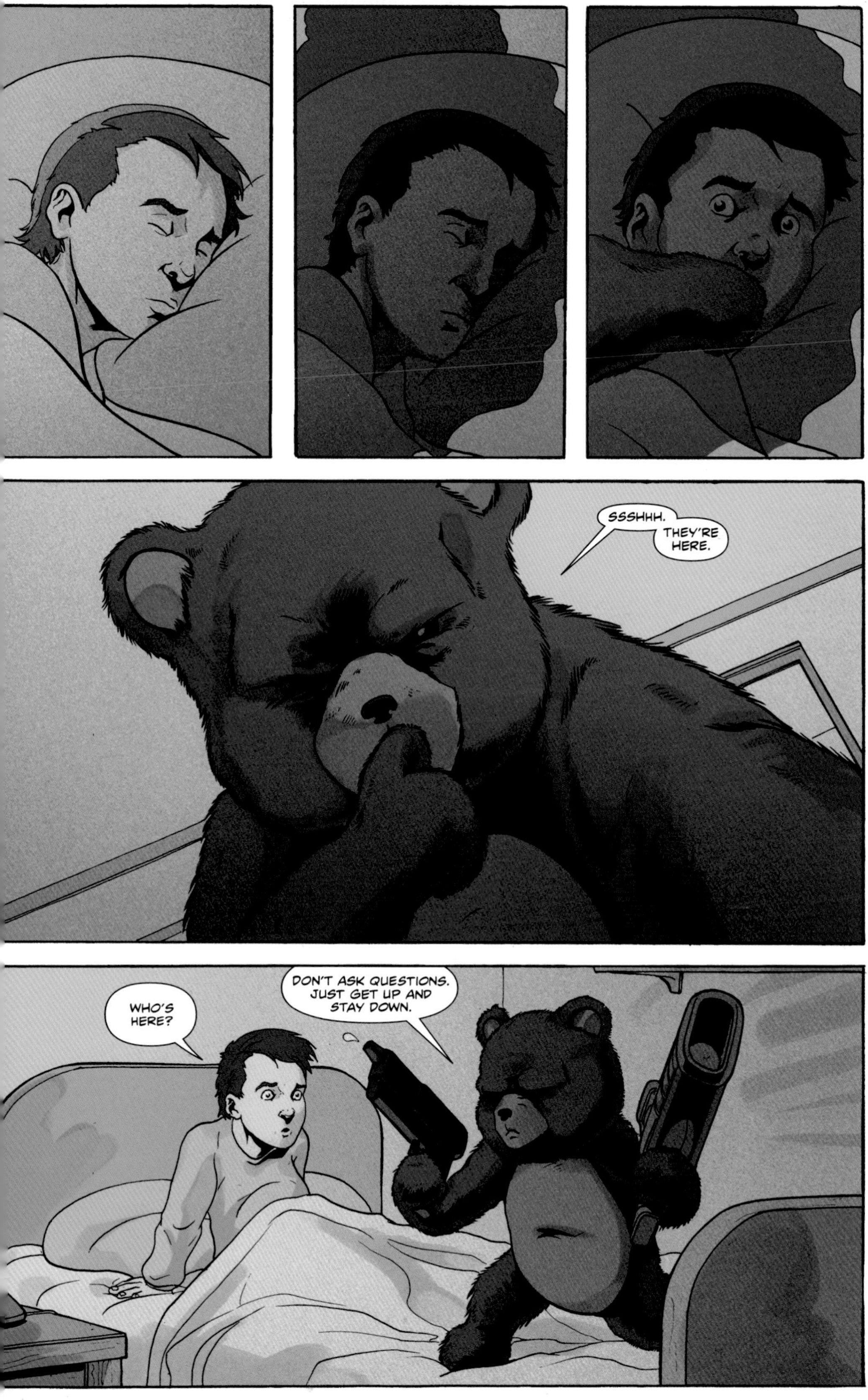
SSSHHH.
THEY'RE HERE.
WHO'S HERE?
DON'T ASK QUESTIONS. JUST GET UP AND STAY DOWN.

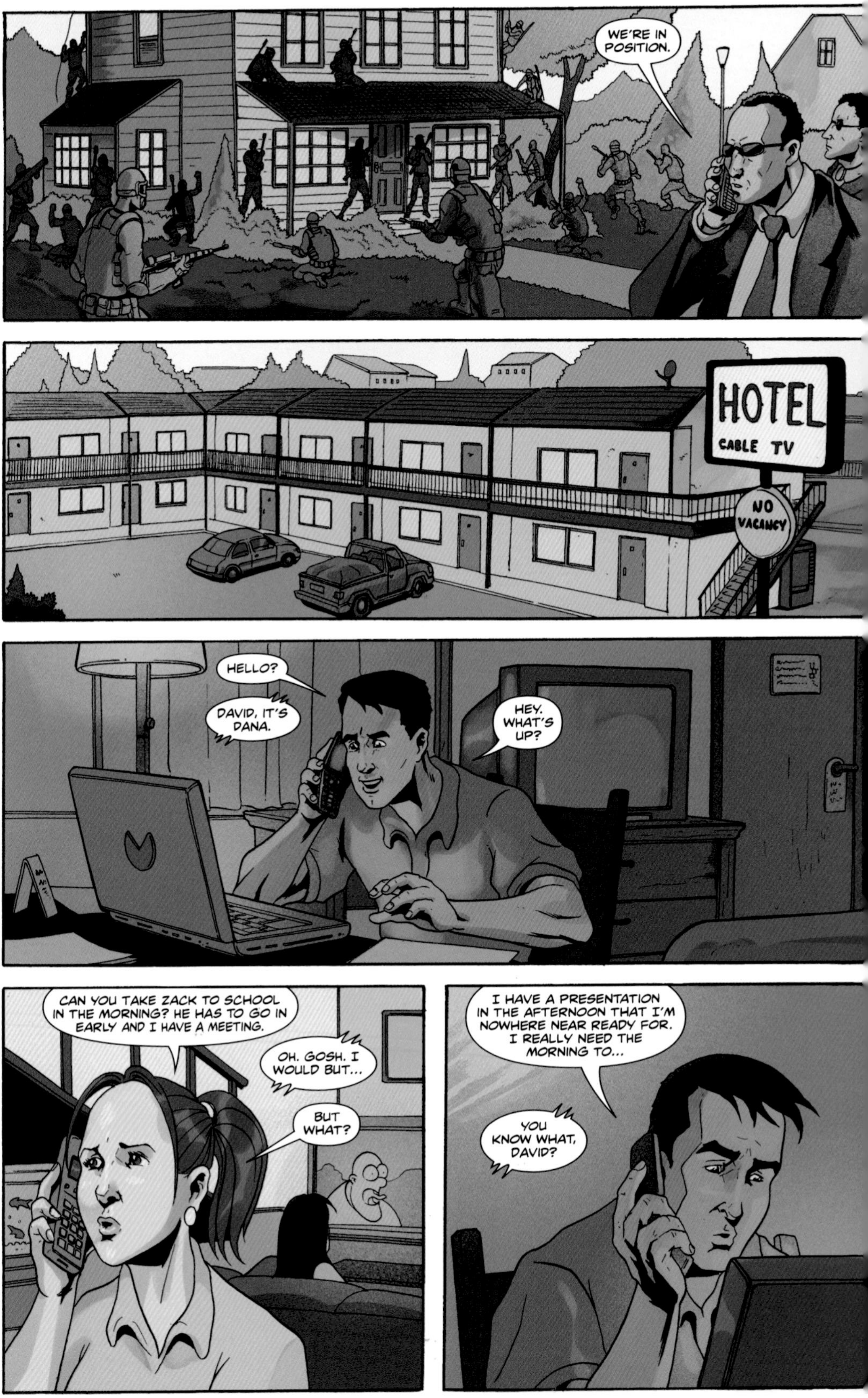
WE'RE IN POSITION.
HOTEL
CABLE TV
NO VACANCY
HELLO?
DAVID, IT'S DANA.
HEY. WHAT'S UP?
CAN YOU TAKE ZACK TO SCHOOL IN THE MORNING? HE HAS TO GO IN EARLY AND I HAVE A MEETING.
OH. GOSH. I WOULD BUT...
BUT WHAT?
I HAVE A PRESENTATION IN THE AFTERNOON THAT I'M NOWHERE NEAR READY FOR. I REALLY NEED THE MORNING TO...
YOU KNOW WHAT, DAVID?

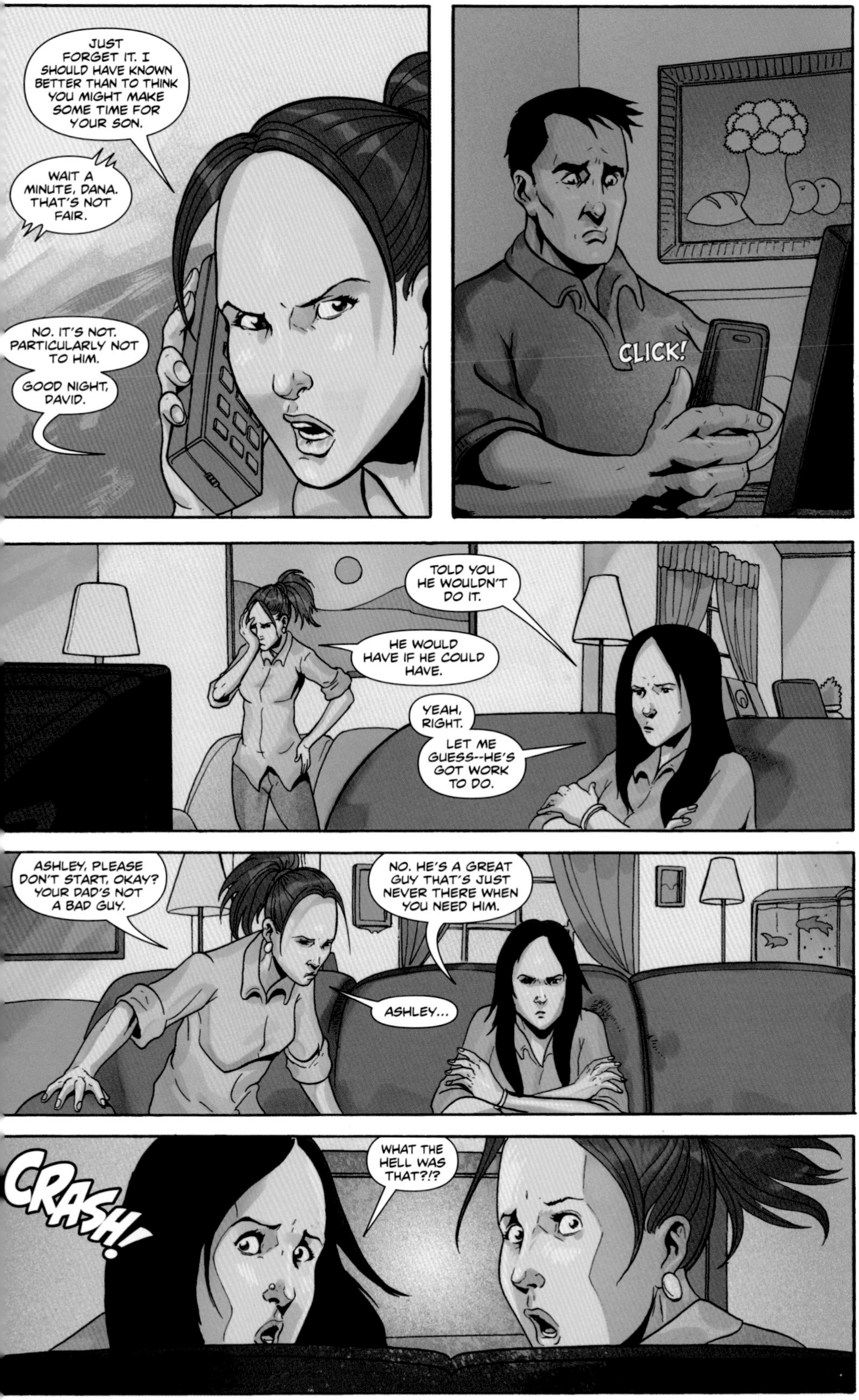
JUST FORGET IT. I SHOULD HAVE KNOWN BETTER THAN TO THINK YOU MIGHT MAKE SOME TIME FOR YOUR SON.
WAIT A MINUTE, DANA. THAT'S NOT FAIR.
NO. IT'S NOT. PARTICULARLY NOT TO HIM.
GOOD NIGHT, DAVID.
CLICK!
TOLD YOU HE WOULDN'T DO IT.
HE WOULD HAVE IF HE COULD HAVE.
YEAH, RIGHT.
LET ME GUESS--HE'S GOT WORK TO DO.
ASHLEY, PLEASE DON'T START, OKAY? YOUR DAD'S NOT A BAD GUY.
NO. HE'S A GREAT GUY THAT'S JUST NEVER THERE WHEN YOU NEED HIM.
ASHLEY...
CRASH!
WHAT THE HELL WAS THAT?!?

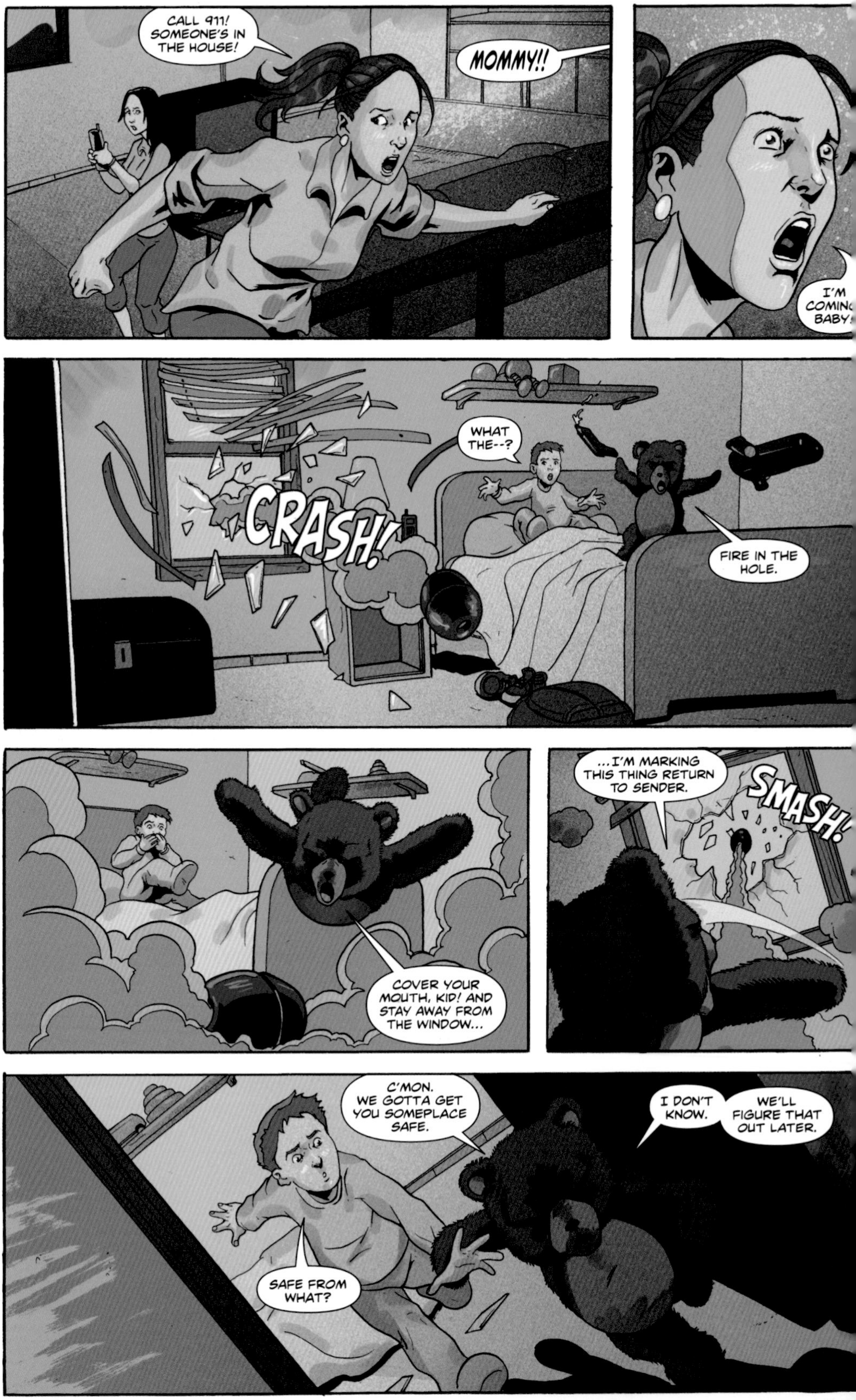
CALL 911! SOMEONE'S IN THE HOUSE!
MOMMY!!
I'M COMIN BABY
WHAT THE--?
CRASH!
FIRE IN THE HOLE.
COVER YOUR MOUTH, KID! AND STAY AWAY FROM THE WINDOW...
...I'M MARKING THIS THING RETURN TO SENDER.
SMASH!
C'MON. WE GOTTA GET YOU SOMEPLACE SAFE.
SAFE FROM WHAT?
I DON'T KNOW.
WE'LL FIGURE THAT OUT LATER.

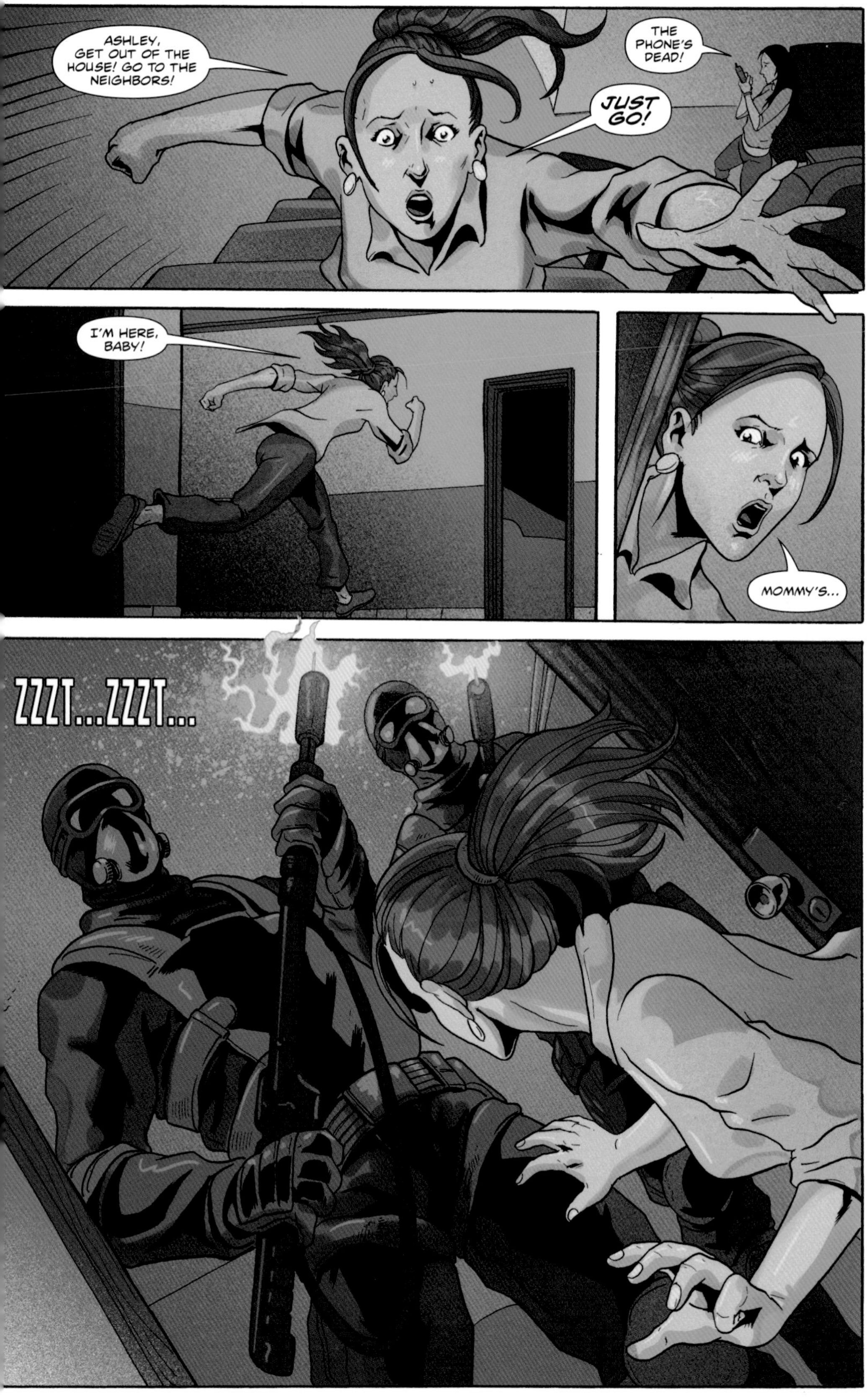
ASHLEY, GET OUT OF THE HOUSE! GO TO THE NEIGHBORS!
THE PHONE'S DEAD!
JUST GO!
I'M HERE, BABY!
MOMMY'S...
ZZZT...ZZZT...

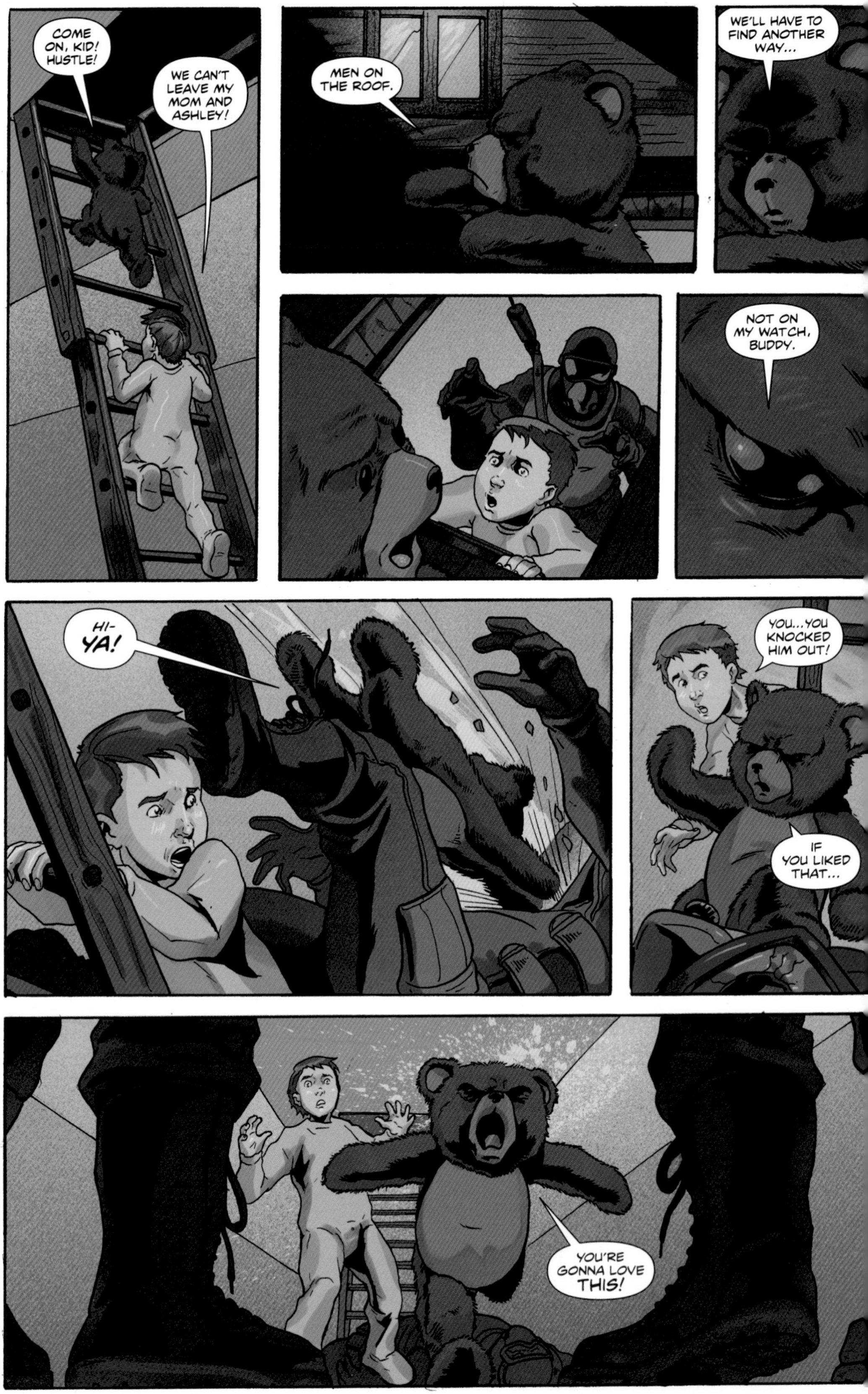
COME ON, KID! HUSTLE!
WE CAN'T LEAVE MY MOM AND ASHLEY!
MEN ON THE ROOF.
WE'LL HAVE TO FIND ANOTHER WAY...
NOT ON MY WATCH, BUDDY.
HI-YA!
YOU...YOU KNOCKED HIM OUT!
IF YOU LIKED THAT...
YOU'RE GONNA LOVE THIS!

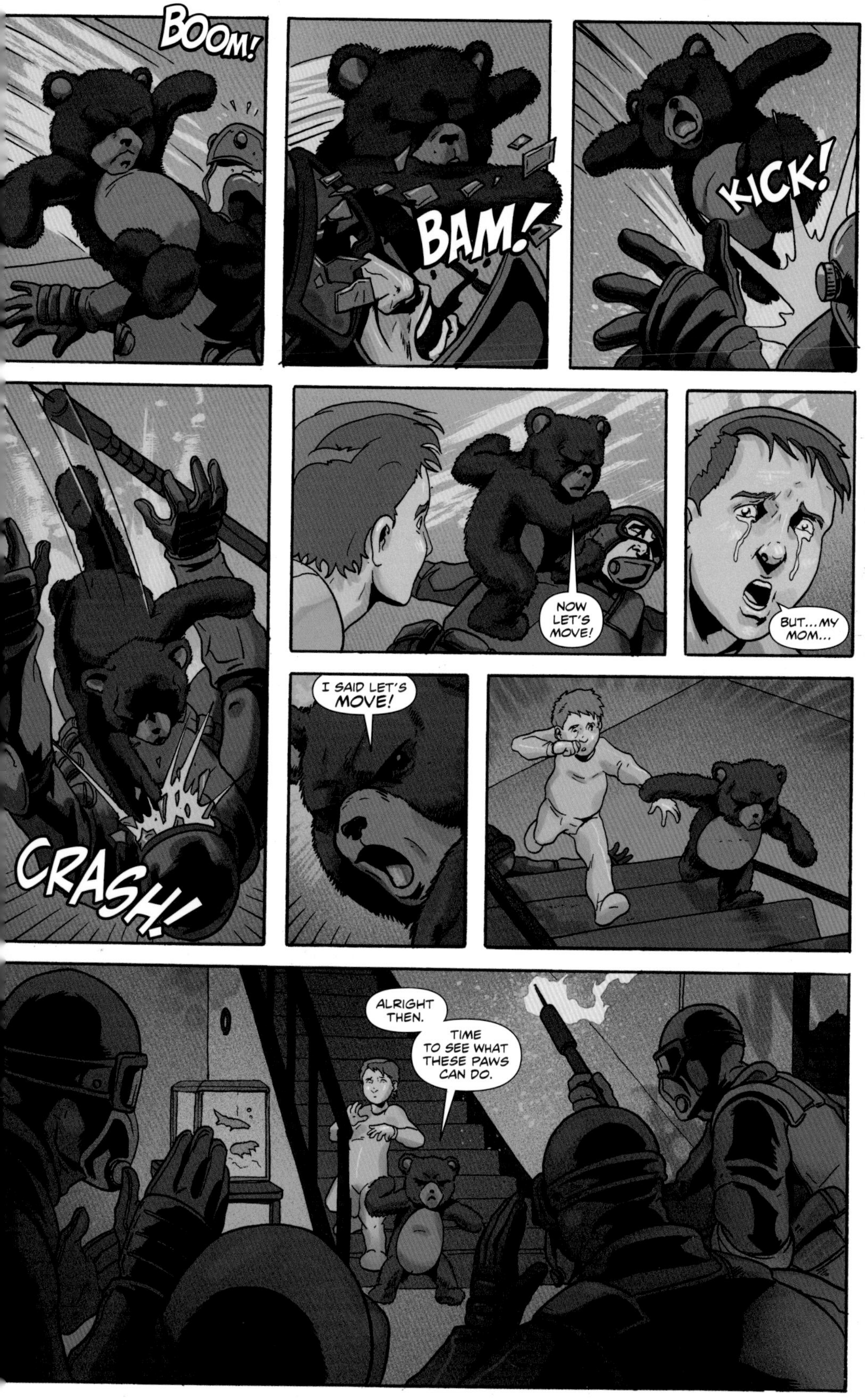
BOOM!
BAM!
KICK!
CRASH!
NOW LET'S MOVE!
BUT...MY MOM...
I SAID LET'S MOVE!
ALRIGHT THEN.
TIME TO SEE WHAT THESE PAWS CAN DO.

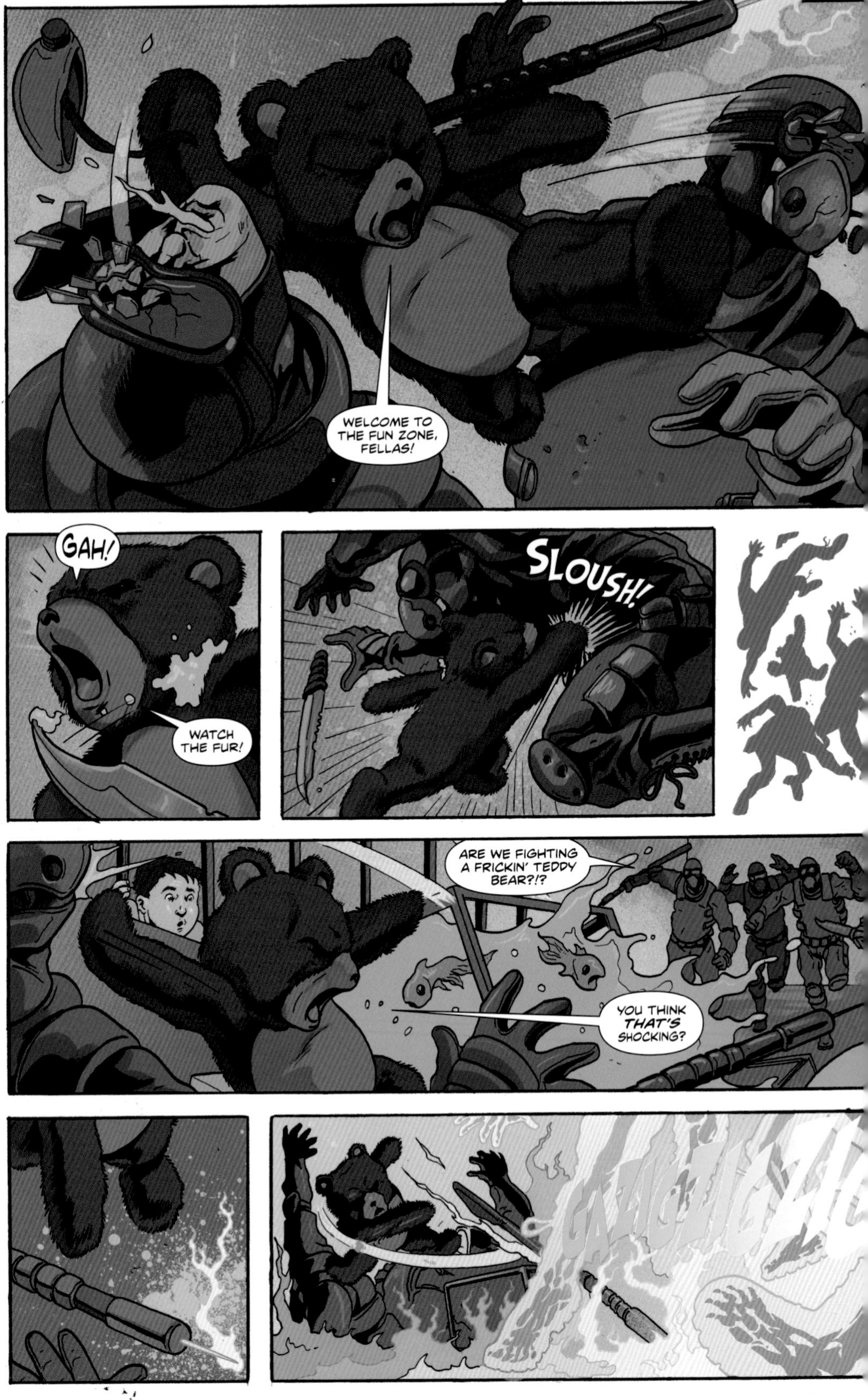
WELCOME TO THE FUN ZONE, FELLAS!
GAH!
WATCH THE FUR!
SLOUSH!
ARE WE FIGHTING A FRICKIN' TEDDY BEAR?!?
YOU THINK THAT'S SHOCKING?

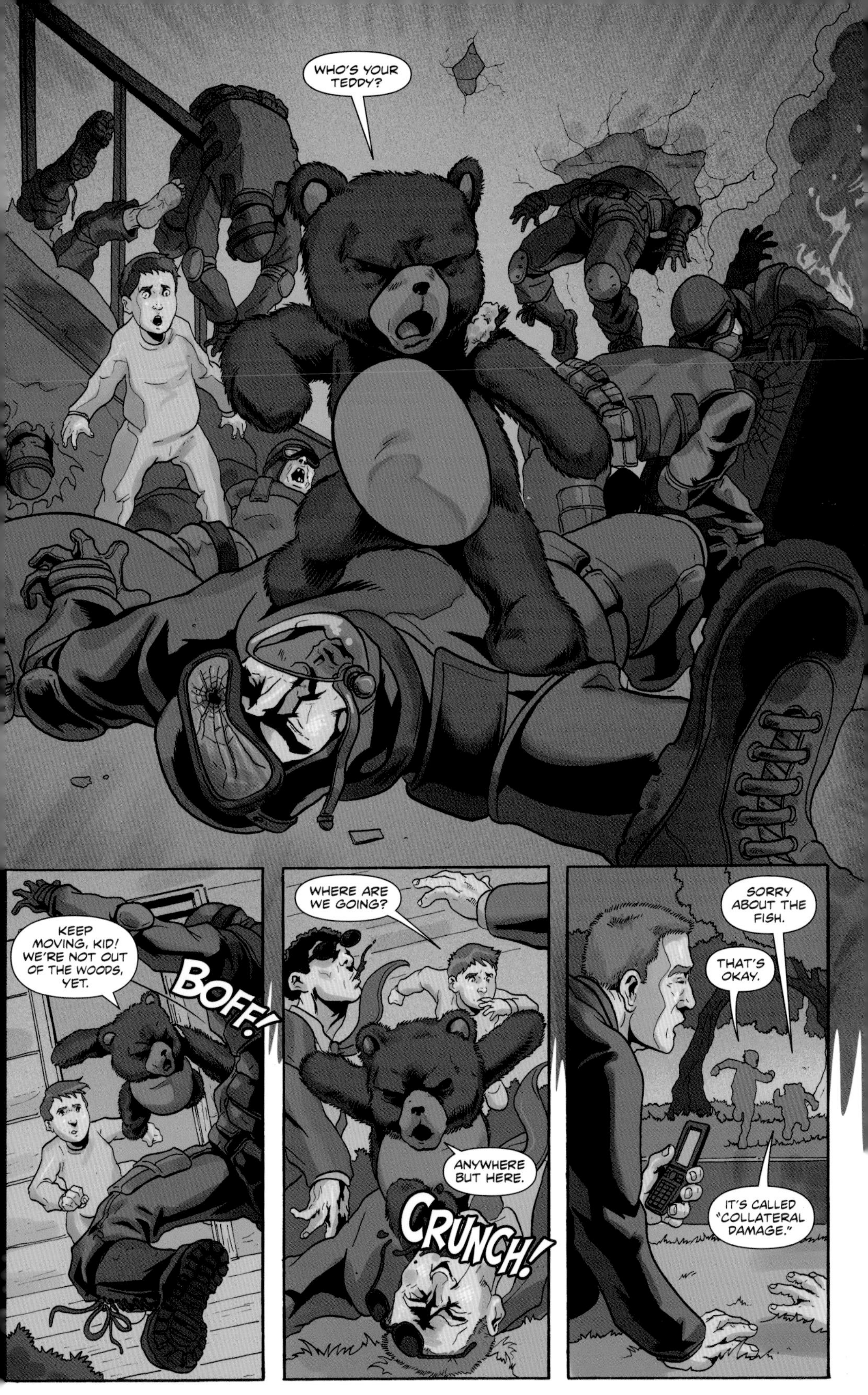
WHO'S YOUR TEDDY?
KEEP MOVING, KID! WE'RE NOT OUT OF THE WOODS, YET.
BOFF!
WHERE ARE WE GOING?
ANYWHERE BUT HERE.
CRUNCH!
SORRY ABOUT THE FISH.
THAT'S OKAY.
IT'S CALLED "COLLATERAL DAMAGE."

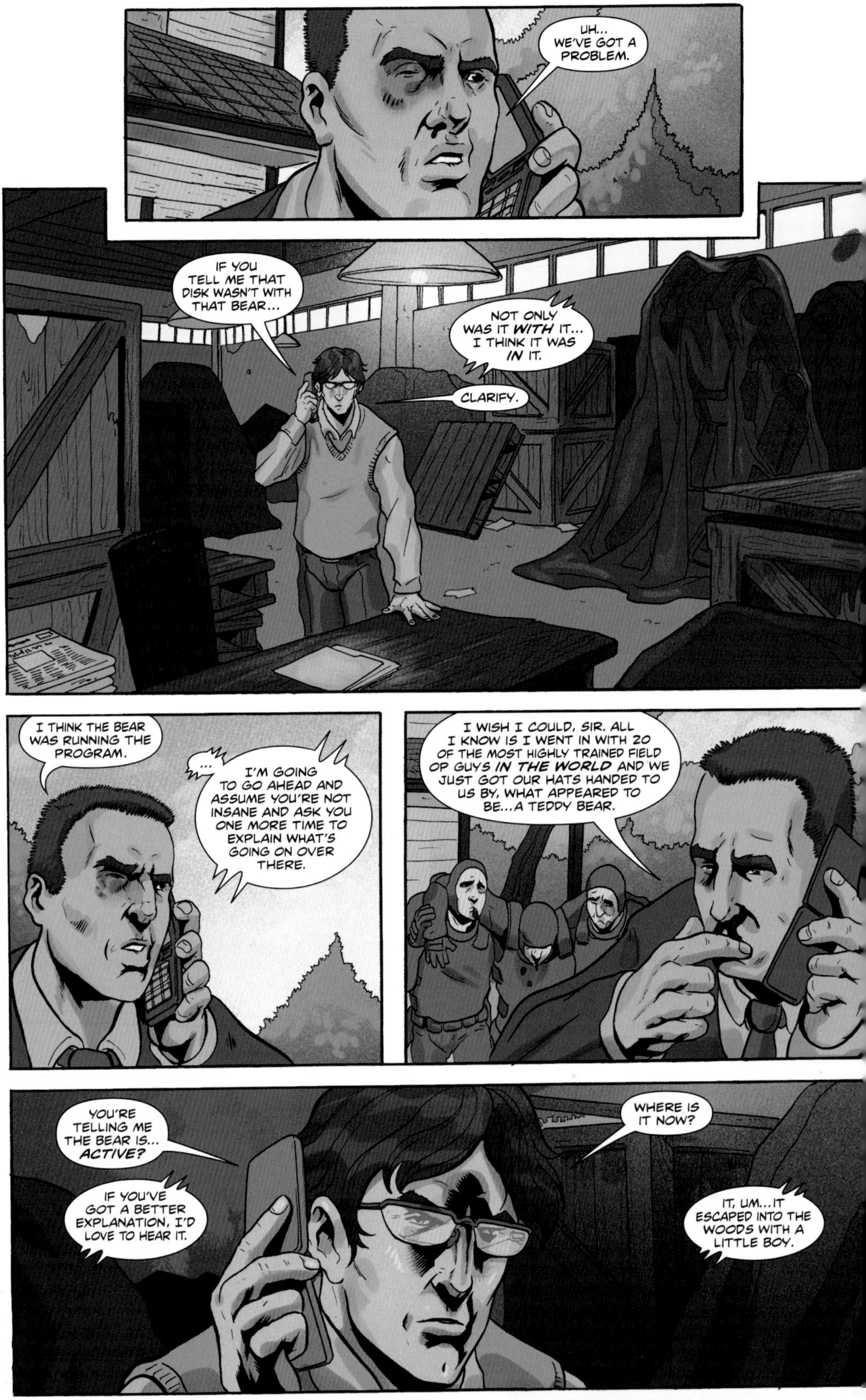
UH... WE'VE GOT A PROBLEM.
IF YOU TELL ME THAT DISK WASN'T WITH THAT BEAR...
NOT ONLY WAS IT *WITH* IT... I THINK IT WAS *IN* IT.
CLARIFY.
I THINK THE BEAR WAS RUNNING THE PROGRAM.
...
I'M GOING TO GO AHEAD AND ASSUME YOU'RE NOT INSANE AND ASK YOU ONE MORE TIME TO EXPLAIN WHAT'S GOING ON OVER THERE.
I WISH I COULD, SIR. ALL I KNOW IS I WENT IN WITH 20 OF THE MOST HIGHLY TRAINED FIELD OP GUYS *IN THE WORLD* AND WE JUST GOT OUR HATS HANDED TO US BY, WHAT APPEARED TO BE...A TEDDY BEAR.
YOU'RE TELLING ME THE BEAR IS... *ACTIVE?*
IF YOU'VE GOT A BETTER EXPLANATION, I'D LOVE TO HEAR IT.
WHERE IS IT NOW?
IT, UM...IT ESCAPED INTO THE WOODS WITH A LITTLE BOY.

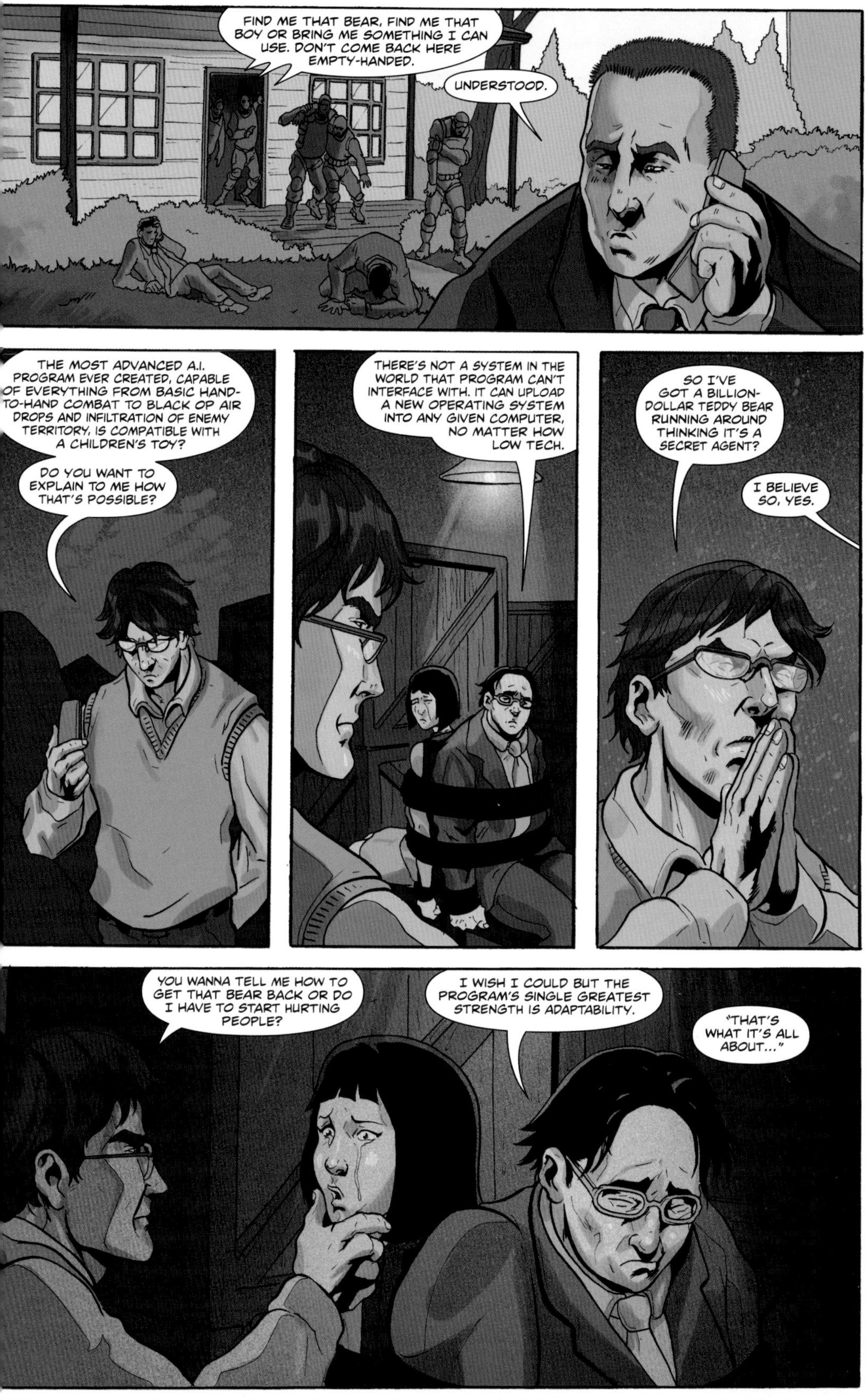
FIND ME THAT BEAR, FIND ME THAT BOY OR BRING ME SOMETHING I CAN USE. DON'T COME BACK HERE EMPTY-HANDED.
UNDERSTOOD.
THE MOST ADVANCED A.I. PROGRAM EVER CREATED, CAPABLE OF EVERYTHING FROM BASIC HAND-TO-HAND COMBAT TO BLACK OP AIR DROPS AND INFILTRATION OF ENEMY TERRITORY, IS COMPATIBLE WITH A CHILDREN'S TOY?
DO YOU WANT TO EXPLAIN TO ME HOW THAT'S POSSIBLE?
THERE'S NOT A SYSTEM IN THE WORLD THAT PROGRAM CAN'T INTERFACE WITH. IT CAN UPLOAD A NEW OPERATING SYSTEM INTO ANY GIVEN COMPUTER, NO MATTER HOW LOW TECH.
SO I'VE GOT A BILLION-DOLLAR TEDDY BEAR RUNNING AROUND THINKING IT'S A SECRET AGENT?
I BELIEVE SO, YES.
YOU WANNA TELL ME HOW TO GET THAT BEAR BACK OR DO I HAVE TO START HURTING PEOPLE?
I WISH I COULD BUT THE PROGRAM'S SINGLE GREATEST STRENGTH IS ADAPTABILITY.
"THAT'S WHAT IT'S ALL ABOUT..."

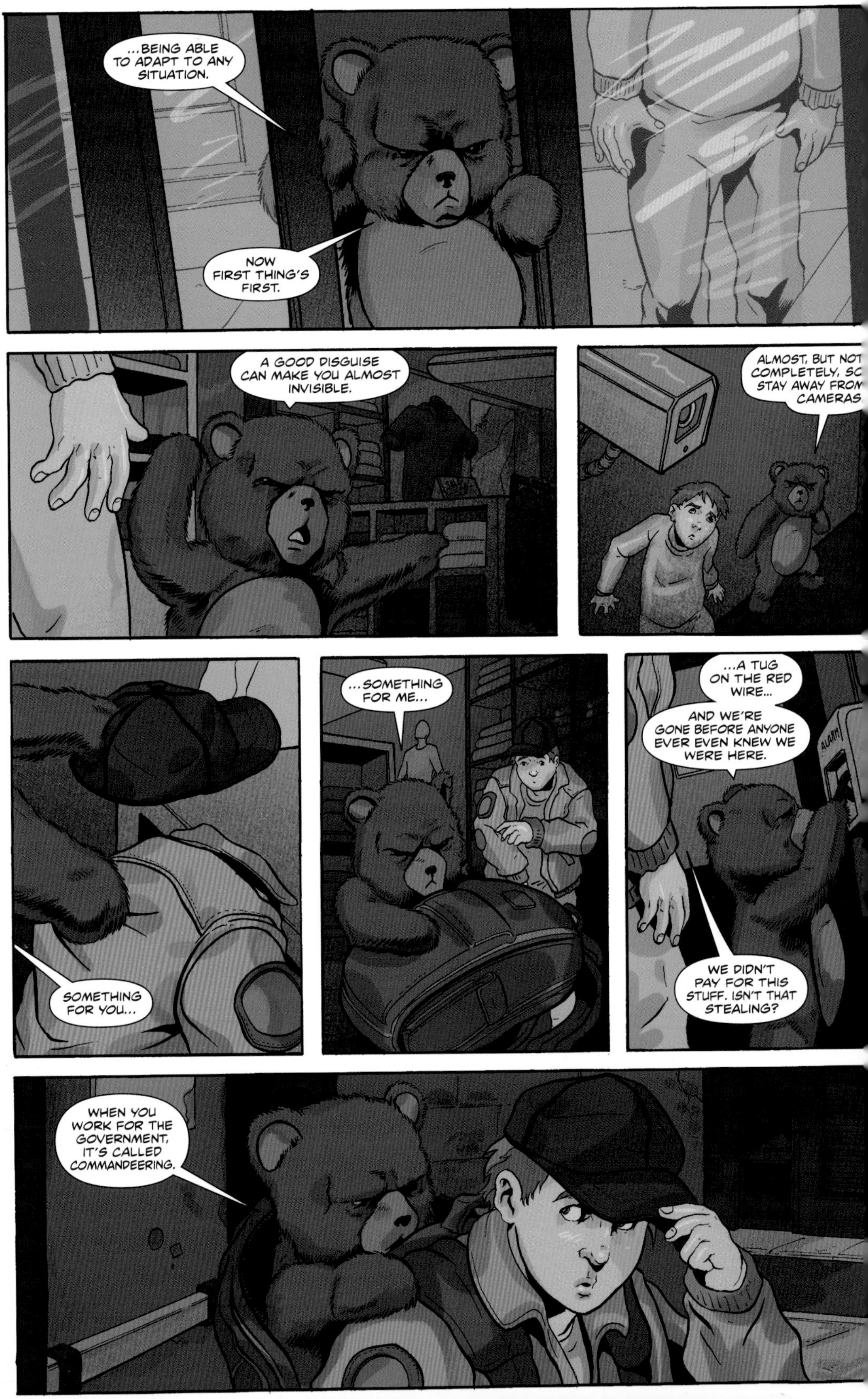
...BEING ABLE TO ADAPT TO ANY SITUATION.
NOW FIRST THING'S FIRST.
A GOOD DISGUISE CAN MAKE YOU ALMOST INVISIBLE.
ALMOST, BUT NOT COMPLETELY, SO STAY AWAY FROM CAMERAS.
SOMETHING FOR YOU...
...SOMETHING FOR ME...
...A TUG ON THE RED WIRE...
AND WE'RE GONE BEFORE ANYONE EVER EVEN KNEW WE WERE HERE.
ALARM
WE DIDN'T PAY FOR THIS STUFF. ISN'T THAT STEALING?
WHEN YOU WORK FOR THE GOVERNMENT, IT'S CALLED COMMANDEERING.

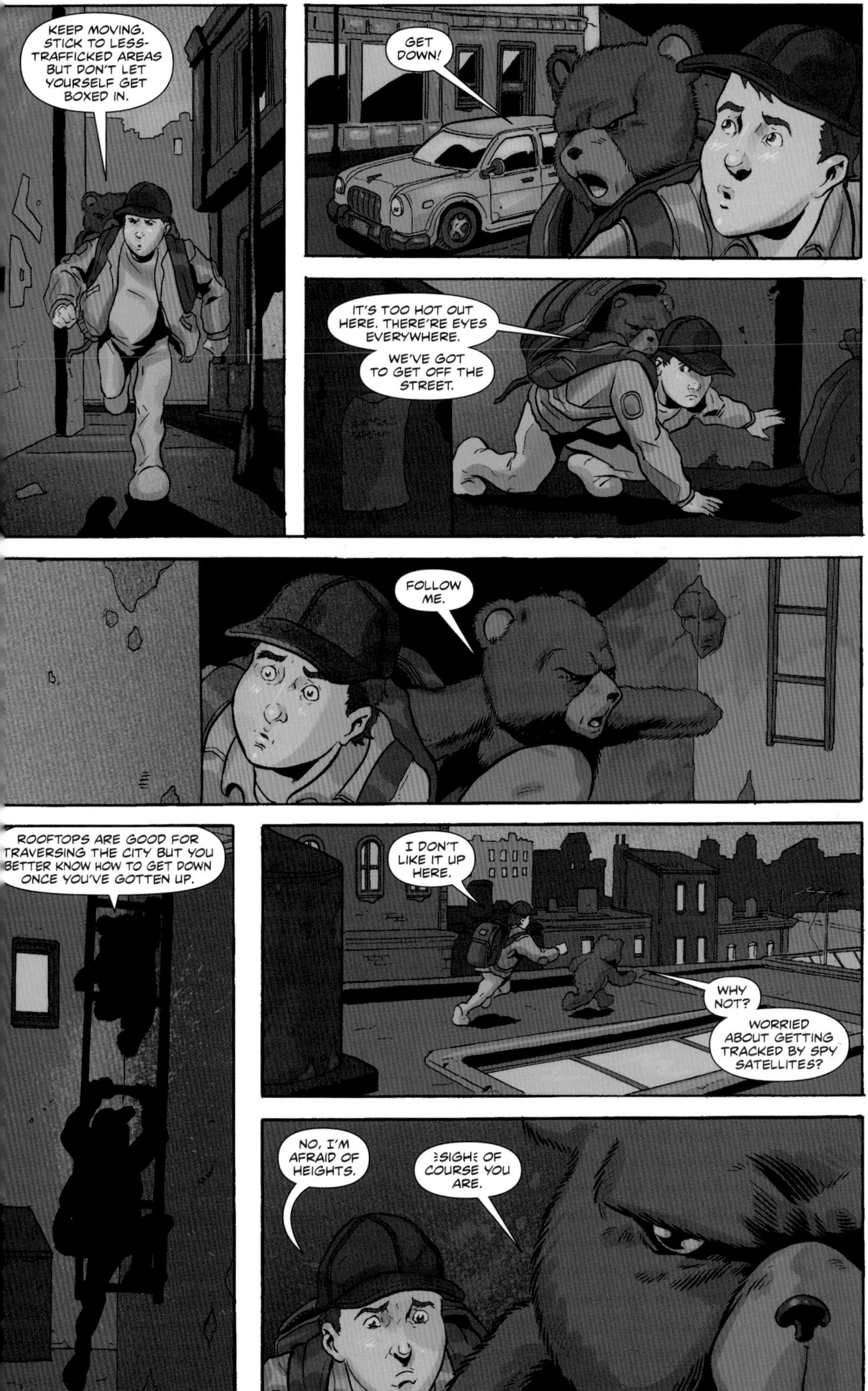
KEEP MOVING. STICK TO LESS-TRAFFICKED AREAS BUT DON'T LET YOURSELF GET BOXED IN.
GET DOWN!
IT'S TOO HOT OUT HERE. THERE'RE EYES EVERYWHERE.
WE'VE GOT TO GET OFF THE STREET.
FOLLOW ME.
ROOFTOPS ARE GOOD FOR TRAVERSING THE CITY BUT YOU BETTER KNOW HOW TO GET DOWN ONCE YOU'VE GOTTEN UP.
I DON'T LIKE IT UP HERE.
WHY NOT?
WORRIED ABOUT GETTING TRACKED BY SPY SATELLITES?
NO, I'M AFRAID OF HEIGHTS.
ƎSIGHƐ OF COURSE YOU ARE.

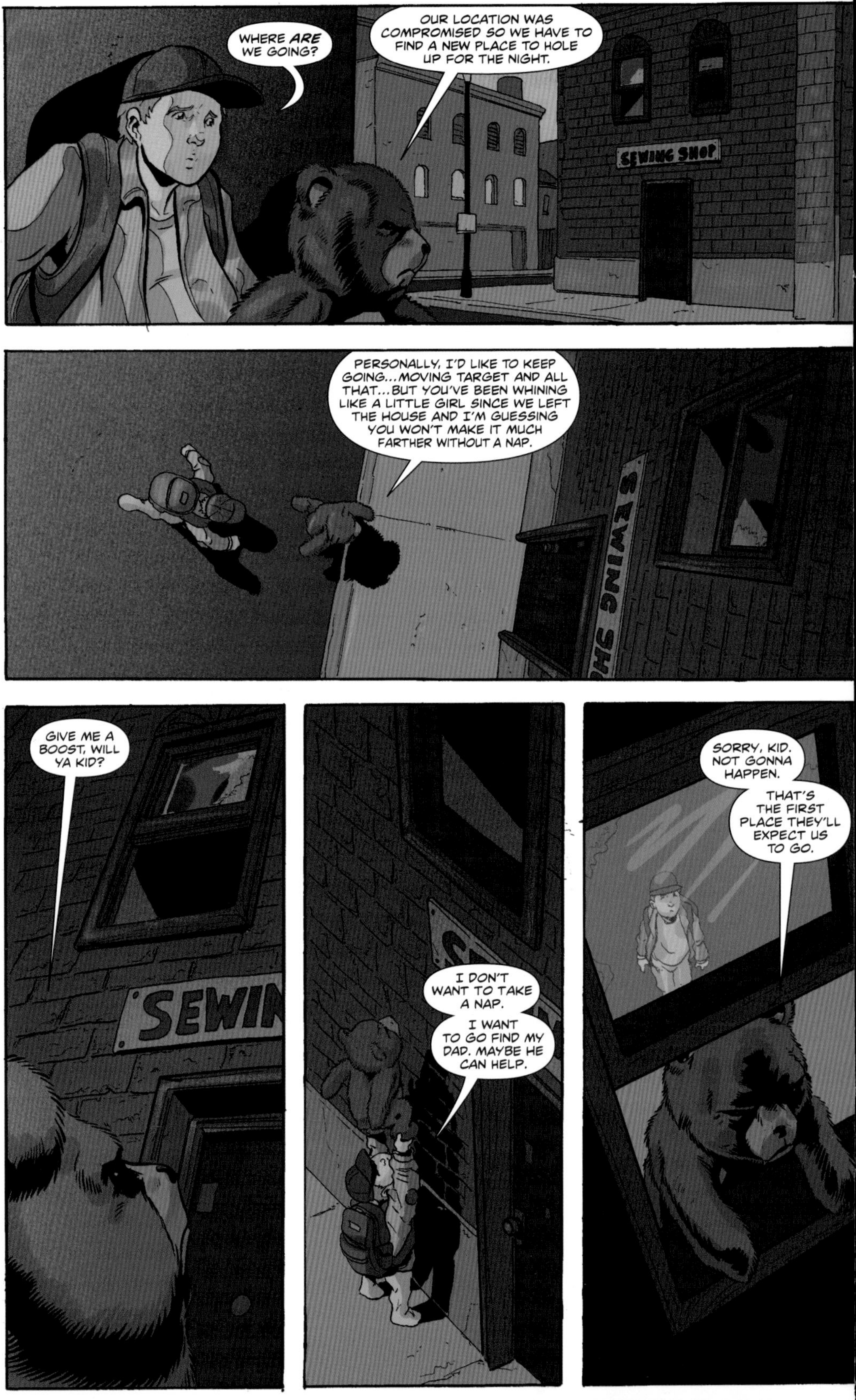
WHERE ARE WE GOING?
OUR LOCATION WAS COMPROMISED SO WE HAVE TO FIND A NEW PLACE TO HOLE UP FOR THE NIGHT.
SEWING SHOP
PERSONALLY, I'D LIKE TO KEEP GOING...MOVING TARGET AND ALL THAT...BUT YOU'VE BEEN WHINING LIKE A LITTLE GIRL SINCE WE LEFT THE HOUSE AND I'M GUESSING YOU WON'T MAKE IT MUCH FARTHER WITHOUT A NAP.
GIVE ME A BOOST, WILL YA KID?
I DON'T WANT TO TAKE A NAP.
I WANT TO GO FIND MY DAD. MAYBE HE CAN HELP.
SORRY, KID. NOT GONNA HAPPEN.
THAT'S THE FIRST PLACE THEY'LL EXPECT US TO GO.

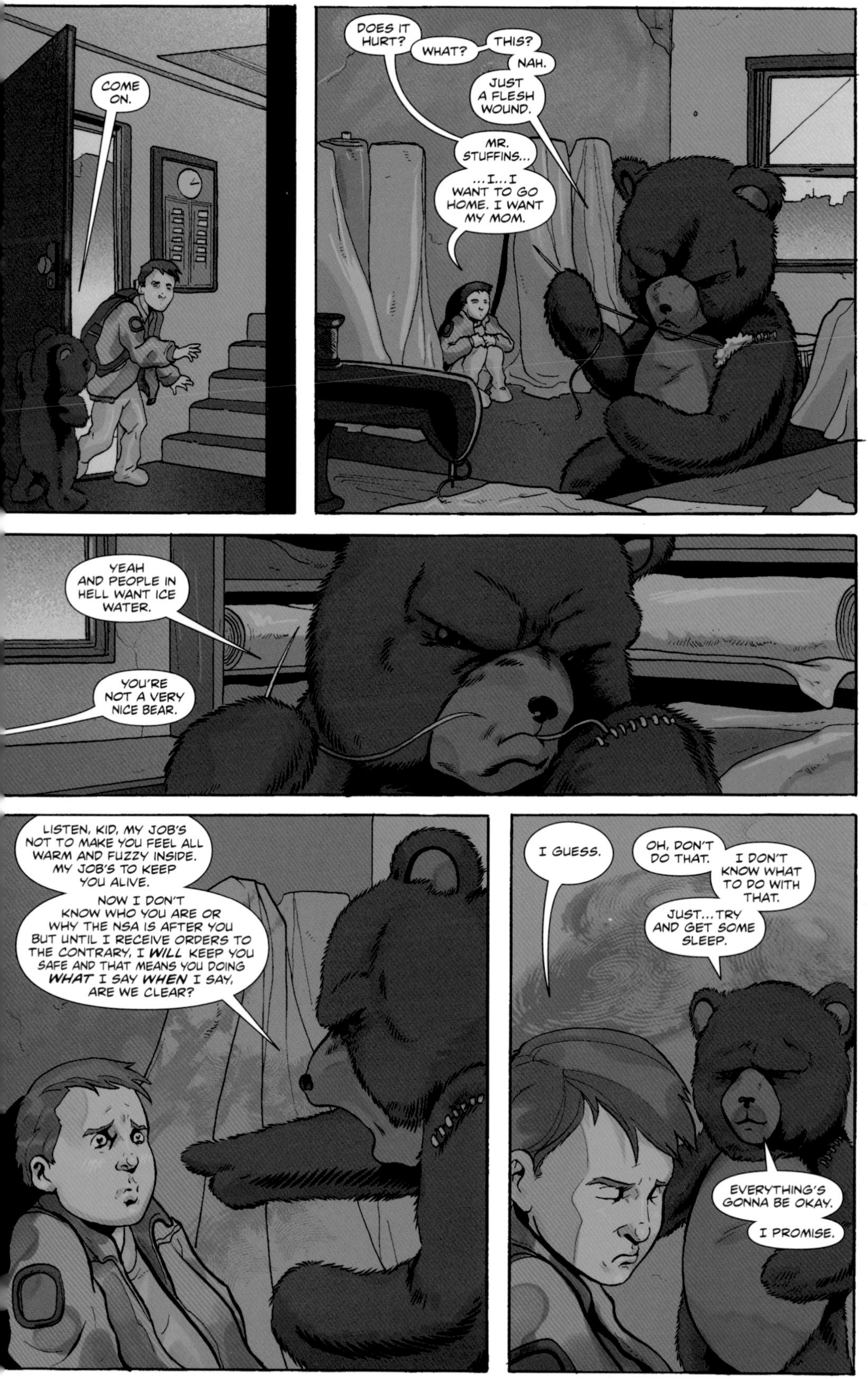
COME ON.
DOES IT HURT?
WHAT?
THIS?
NAH.
JUST A FLESH WOUND.
MR. STUFFINS...
...I...I WANT TO GO HOME. I WANT MY MOM.
YEAH AND PEOPLE IN HELL WANT ICE WATER.
YOU'RE NOT A VERY NICE BEAR.
LISTEN, KID, MY JOB'S NOT TO MAKE YOU FEEL ALL WARM AND FUZZY INSIDE. MY JOB'S TO KEEP YOU ALIVE.
NOW I DON'T KNOW WHO YOU ARE OR WHY THE NSA IS AFTER YOU BUT UNTIL I RECEIVE ORDERS TO THE CONTRARY, I WILL KEEP YOU SAFE AND THAT MEANS YOU DOING WHAT I SAY WHEN I SAY, ARE WE CLEAR?
I GUESS.
OH, DON'T DO THAT.
I DON'T KNOW WHAT TO DO WITH THAT.
JUST...TRY AND GET SOME SLEEP.
EVERYTHING'S GONNA BE OKAY.
I PROMISE.

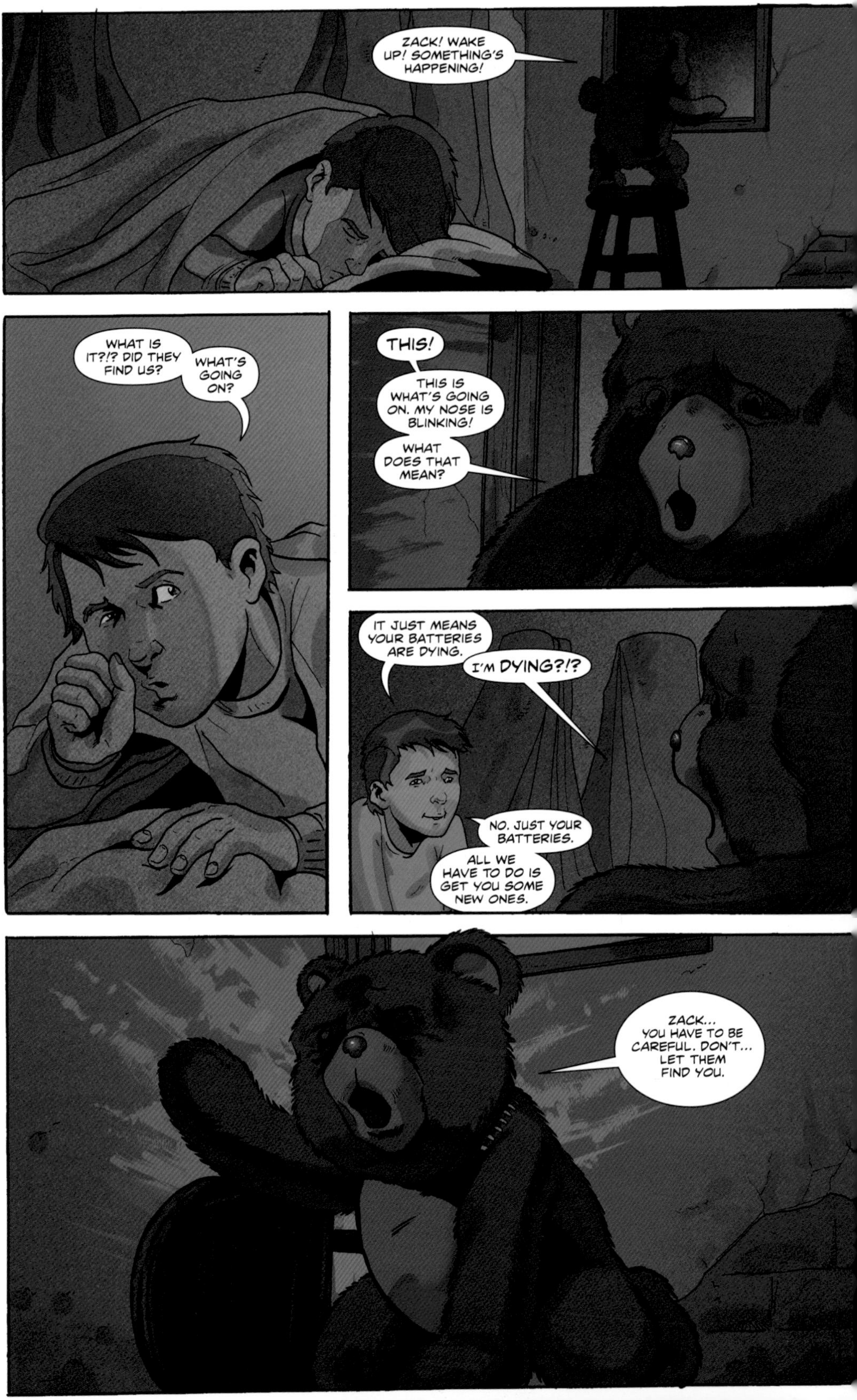
ZACK! WAKE UP! SOMETHING'S HAPPENING!
WHAT IS IT?!? DID THEY FIND US?
WHAT'S GOING ON?
THIS!
THIS IS WHAT'S GOING ON. MY NOSE IS BLINKING!
WHAT DOES THAT MEAN?
IT JUST MEANS YOUR BATTERIES ARE DYING.
I'M DYING?!?
NO. JUST YOUR BATTERIES.
ALL WE HAVE TO DO IS GET YOU SOME NEW ONES.
ZACK... YOU HAVE TO BE CAREFUL. DON'T... LET THEM FIND YOU.

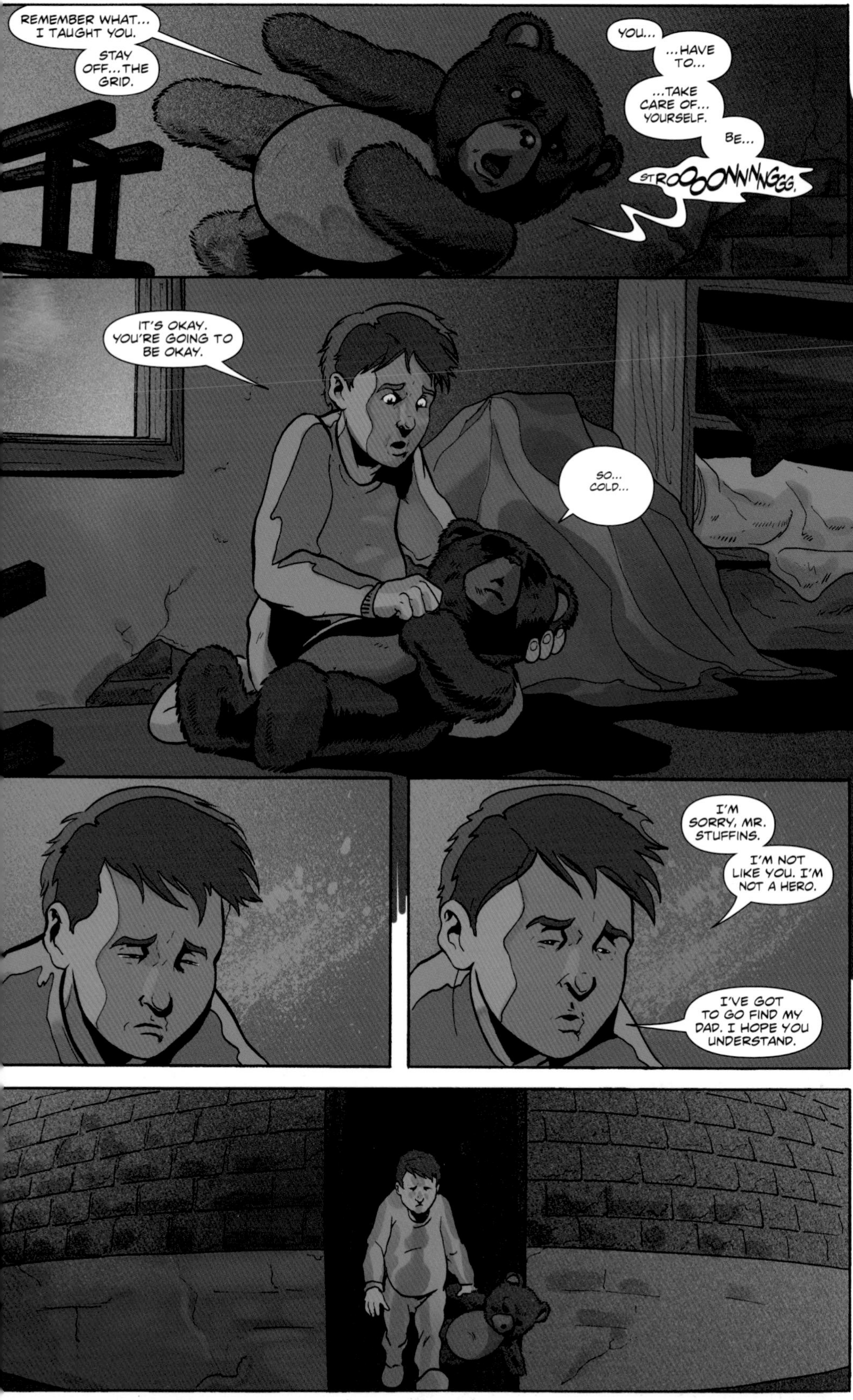
REMEMBER WHAT... I TAUGHT YOU.
STAY OFF...THE GRID.
YOU...
...HAVE TO...
...TAKE CARE OF... YOURSELF.
BE...
STROOOOONNNNGGG.
IT'S OKAY. YOU'RE GOING TO BE OKAY.
SO... COLD...
I'M SORRY, MR. STUFFINS.
I'M NOT LIKE YOU. I'M NOT A HERO.
I'VE GOT TO GO FIND MY DAD. I HOPE YOU UNDERSTAND.

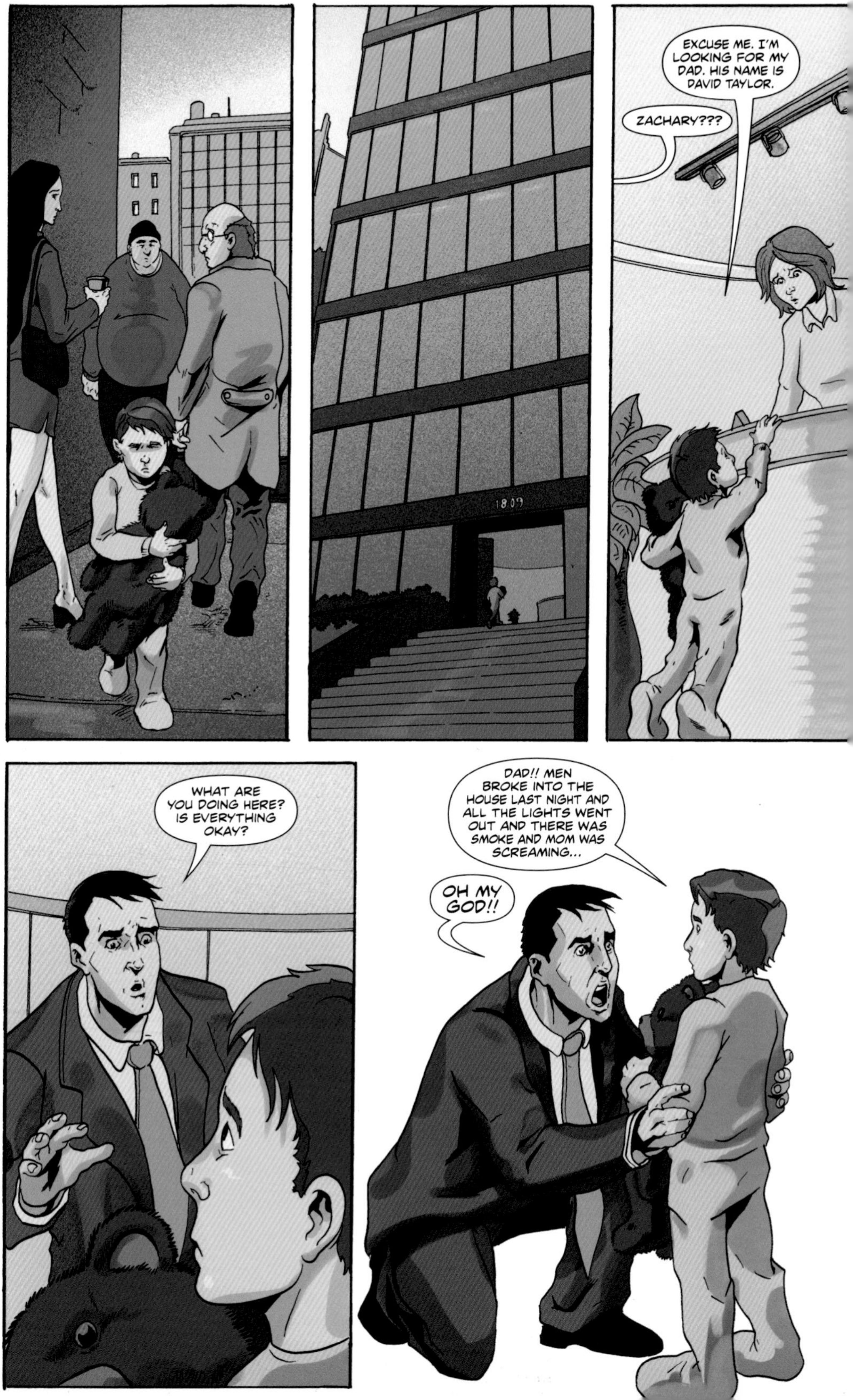
1809
EXCUSE ME. I'M LOOKING FOR MY DAD. HIS NAME IS DAVID TAYLOR.
ZACHARY???
WHAT ARE YOU DOING HERE? IS EVERYTHING OKAY?
DAD!! MEN BROKE INTO THE HOUSE LAST NIGHT AND ALL THE LIGHTS WENT OUT AND THERE WAS SMOKE AND MOM WAS SCREAMING...
OH MY GOD!!

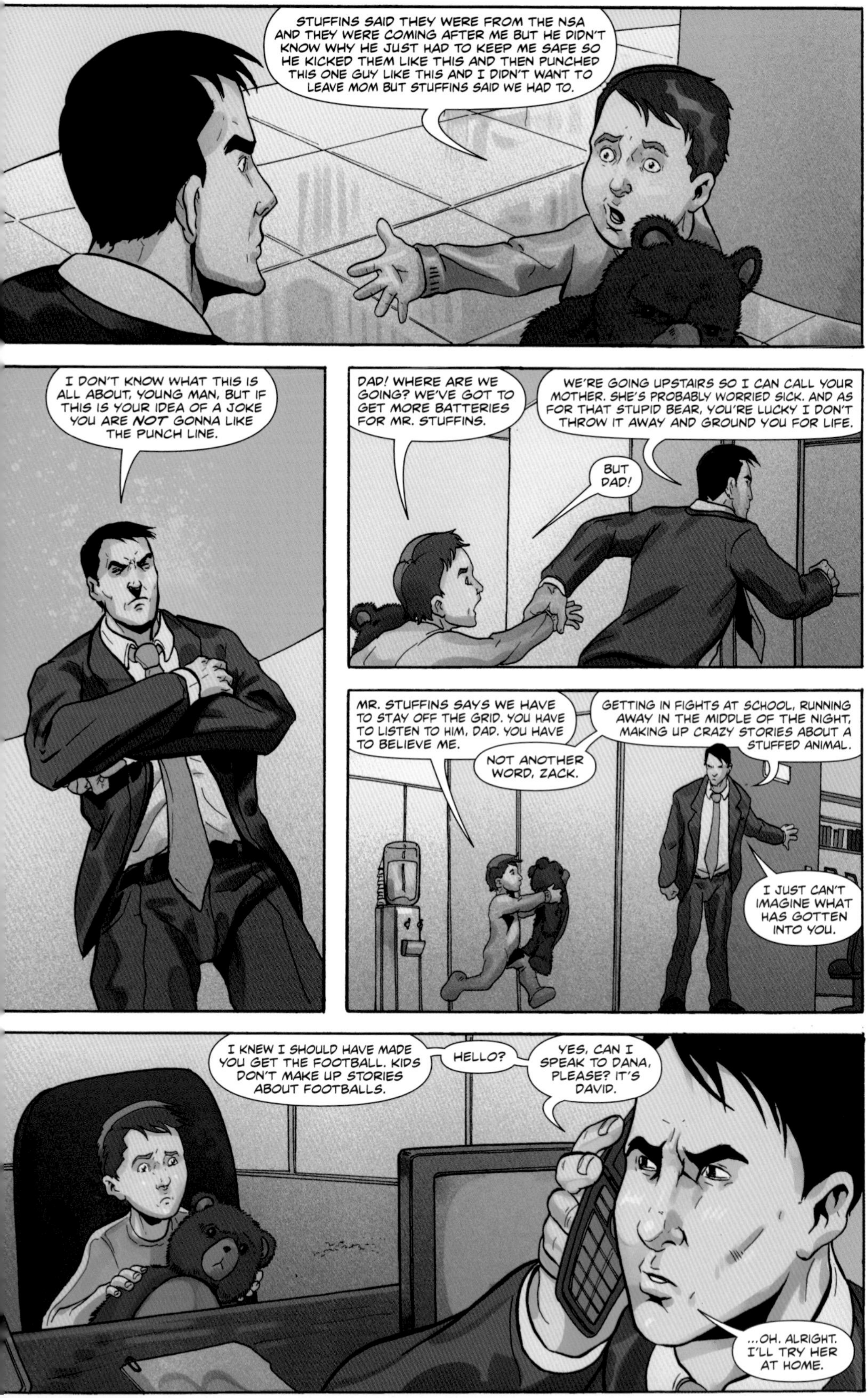
STUFFINS SAID THEY WERE FROM THE NSA AND THEY WERE COMING AFTER ME BUT HE DIDN'T KNOW WHY HE JUST HAD TO KEEP ME SAFE SO HE KICKED THEM LIKE THIS AND THEN PUNCHED THIS ONE GUY LIKE THIS AND I DIDN'T WANT TO LEAVE MOM BUT STUFFINS SAID WE HAD TO.
I DON'T KNOW WHAT THIS IS ALL ABOUT, YOUNG MAN, BUT IF THIS IS YOUR IDEA OF A JOKE YOU ARE NOT GONNA LIKE THE PUNCH LINE.
DAD! WHERE ARE WE GOING? WE'VE GOT TO GET MORE BATTERIES FOR MR. STUFFINS.
WE'RE GOING UPSTAIRS SO I CAN CALL YOUR MOTHER. SHE'S PROBABLY WORRIED SICK. AND AS FOR THAT STUPID BEAR, YOU'RE LUCKY I DON'T THROW IT AWAY AND GROUND YOU FOR LIFE.
BUT DAD!
MR. STUFFINS SAYS WE HAVE TO STAY OFF THE GRID. YOU HAVE TO LISTEN TO HIM, DAD. YOU HAVE TO BELIEVE ME.
NOT ANOTHER WORD, ZACK.
GETTING IN FIGHTS AT SCHOOL, RUNNING AWAY IN THE MIDDLE OF THE NIGHT, MAKING UP CRAZY STORIES ABOUT A STUFFED ANIMAL.
I JUST CAN'T IMAGINE WHAT HAS GOTTEN INTO YOU.
I KNEW I SHOULD HAVE MADE YOU GET THE FOOTBALL. KIDS DON'T MAKE UP STORIES ABOUT FOOTBALLS.
HELLO?
YES, CAN I SPEAK TO DANA, PLEASE? IT'S DAVID.
...OH. ALRIGHT. I'LL TRY HER AT HOME.

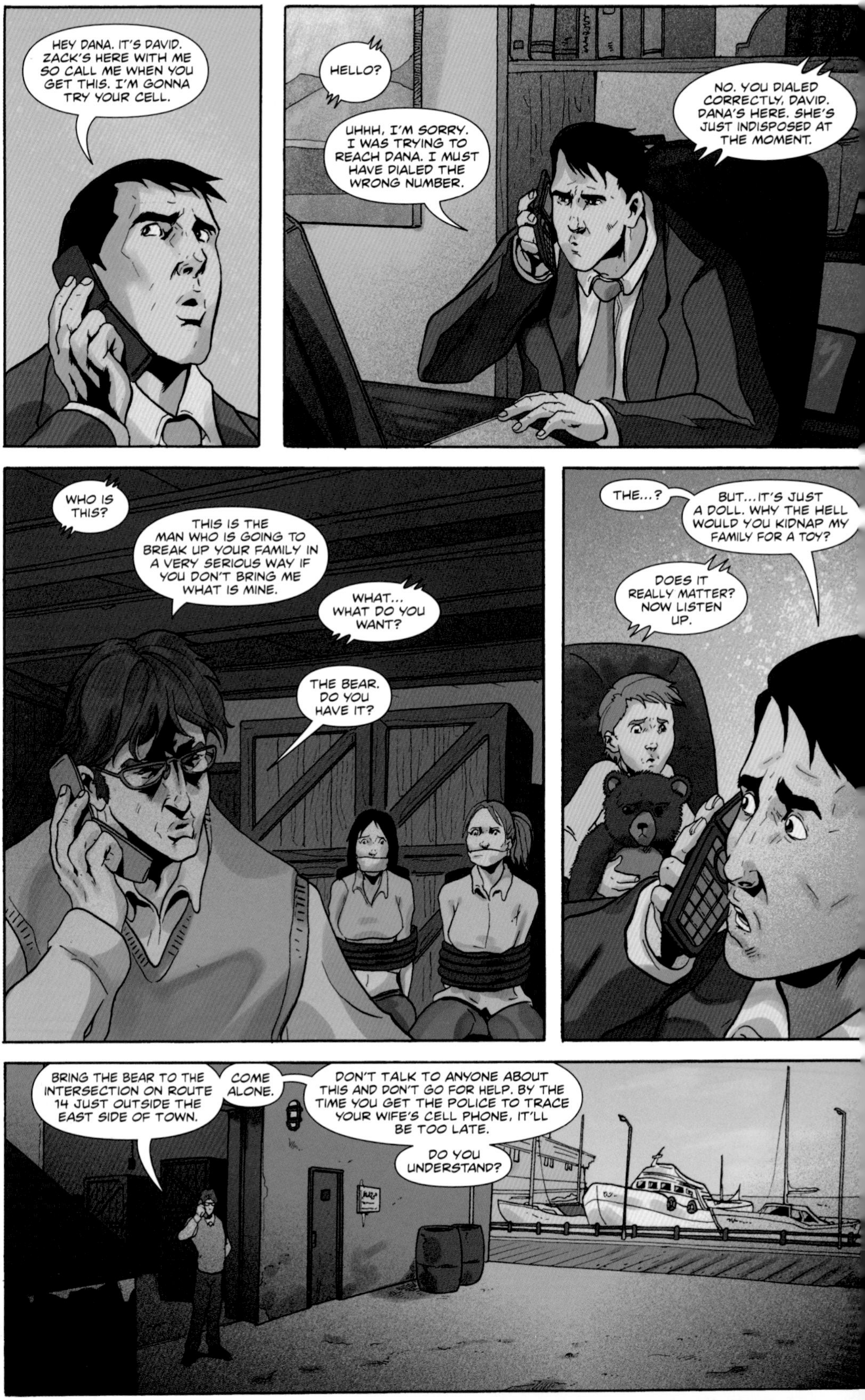
HEY DANA. IT'S DAVID. ZACK'S HERE WITH ME SO CALL ME WHEN YOU GET THIS. I'M GONNA TRY YOUR CELL.
HELLO?
UHHH, I'M SORRY. I WAS TRYING TO REACH DANA. I MUST HAVE DIALED THE WRONG NUMBER.
NO. YOU DIALED CORRECTLY, DAVID. DANA'S HERE. SHE'S JUST INDISPOSED AT THE MOMENT.
WHO IS THIS?
THIS IS THE MAN WHO IS GOING TO BREAK UP YOUR FAMILY IN A VERY SERIOUS WAY IF YOU DON'T BRING ME WHAT IS MINE.
WHAT... WHAT DO YOU WANT?
THE BEAR. DO YOU HAVE IT?
THE...?
BUT...IT'S JUST A DOLL. WHY THE HELL WOULD YOU KIDNAP MY FAMILY FOR A TOY?
DOES IT REALLY MATTER? NOW LISTEN UP.
BRING THE BEAR TO THE INTERSECTION ON ROUTE 14 JUST OUTSIDE THE EAST SIDE OF TOWN.
COME ALONE.
DON'T TALK TO ANYONE ABOUT THIS AND DON'T GO FOR HELP. BY THE TIME YOU GET THE POLICE TO TRACE YOUR WIFE'S CELL PHONE, IT'LL BE TOO LATE.
DO YOU UNDERSTAND?

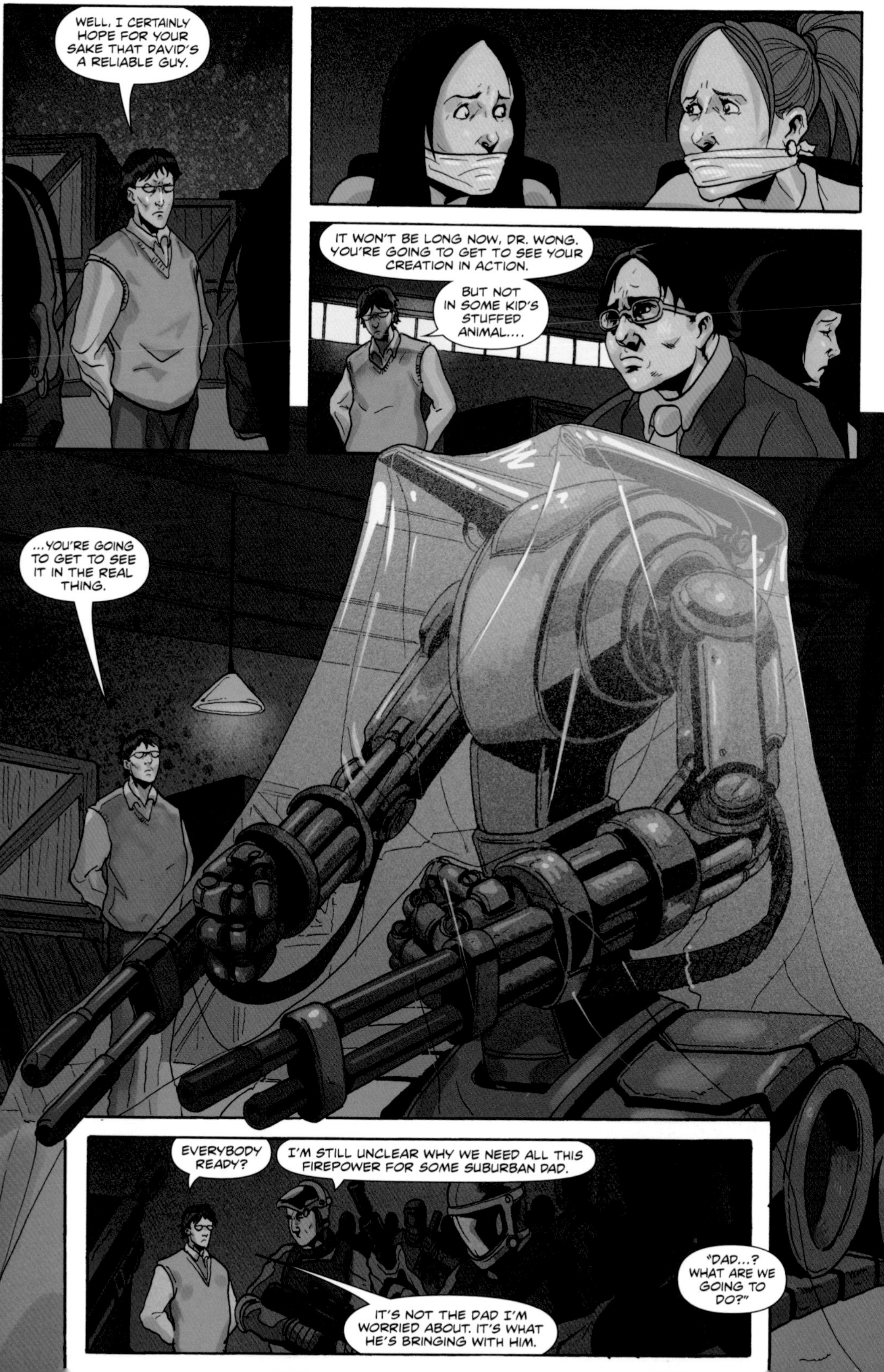
WELL, I CERTAINLY HOPE FOR YOUR SAKE THAT DAVID'S A RELIABLE GUY.
IT WON'T BE LONG NOW, DR. WONG. YOU'RE GOING TO GET TO SEE YOUR CREATION IN ACTION.
BUT NOT IN SOME KID'S STUFFED ANIMAL....
...YOU'RE GOING TO GET TO SEE IT IN THE REAL THING.
EVERYBODY READY?
I'M STILL UNCLEAR WHY WE NEED ALL THIS FIREPOWER FOR SOME SUBURBAN DAD.
IT'S NOT THE DAD I'M WORRIED ABOUT. IT'S WHAT HE'S BRINGING WITH HIM.
"DAD...? WHAT ARE WE GOING TO DO?"

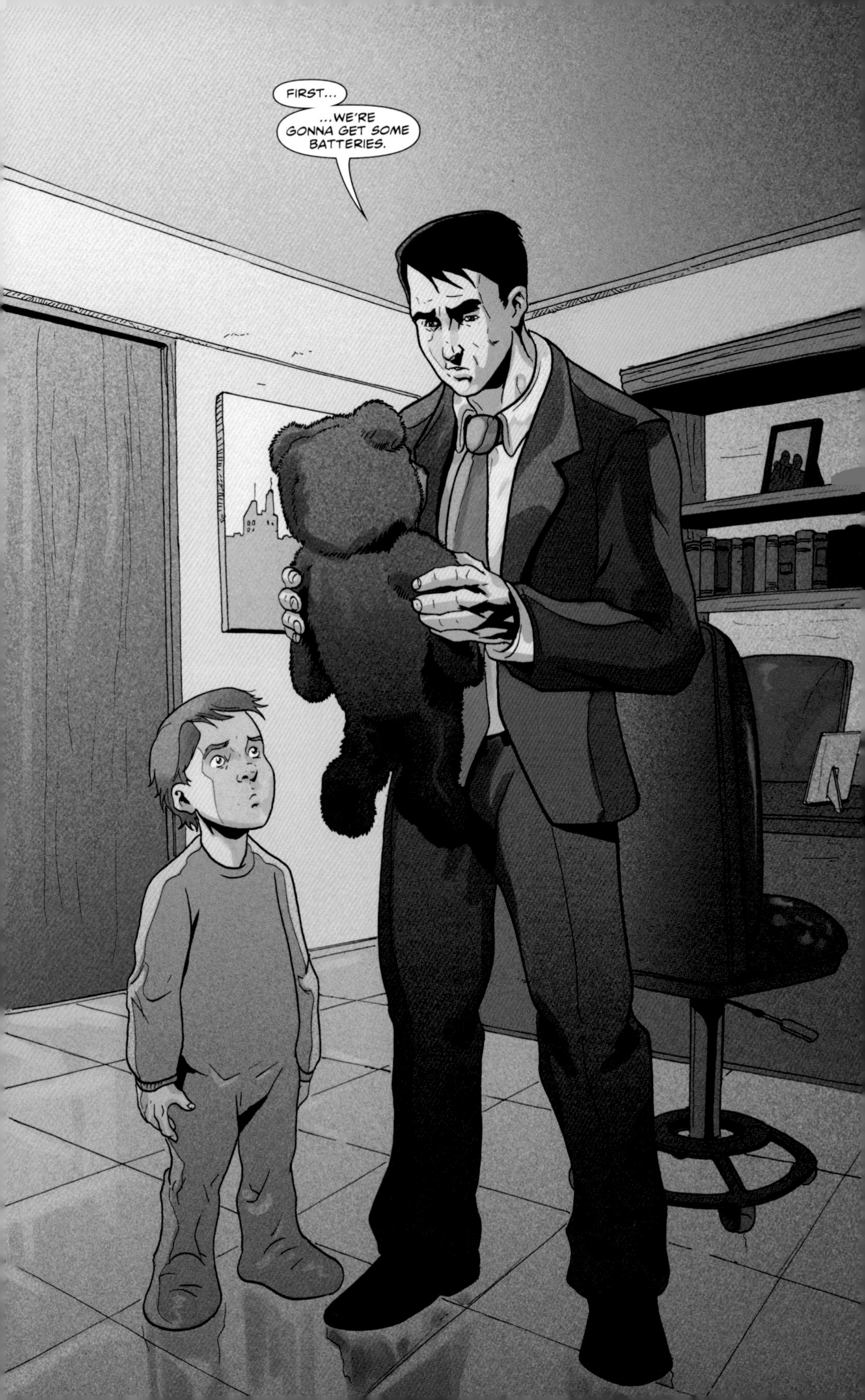
FIRST...
...WE'RE GONNA GET SOME BATTERIES.

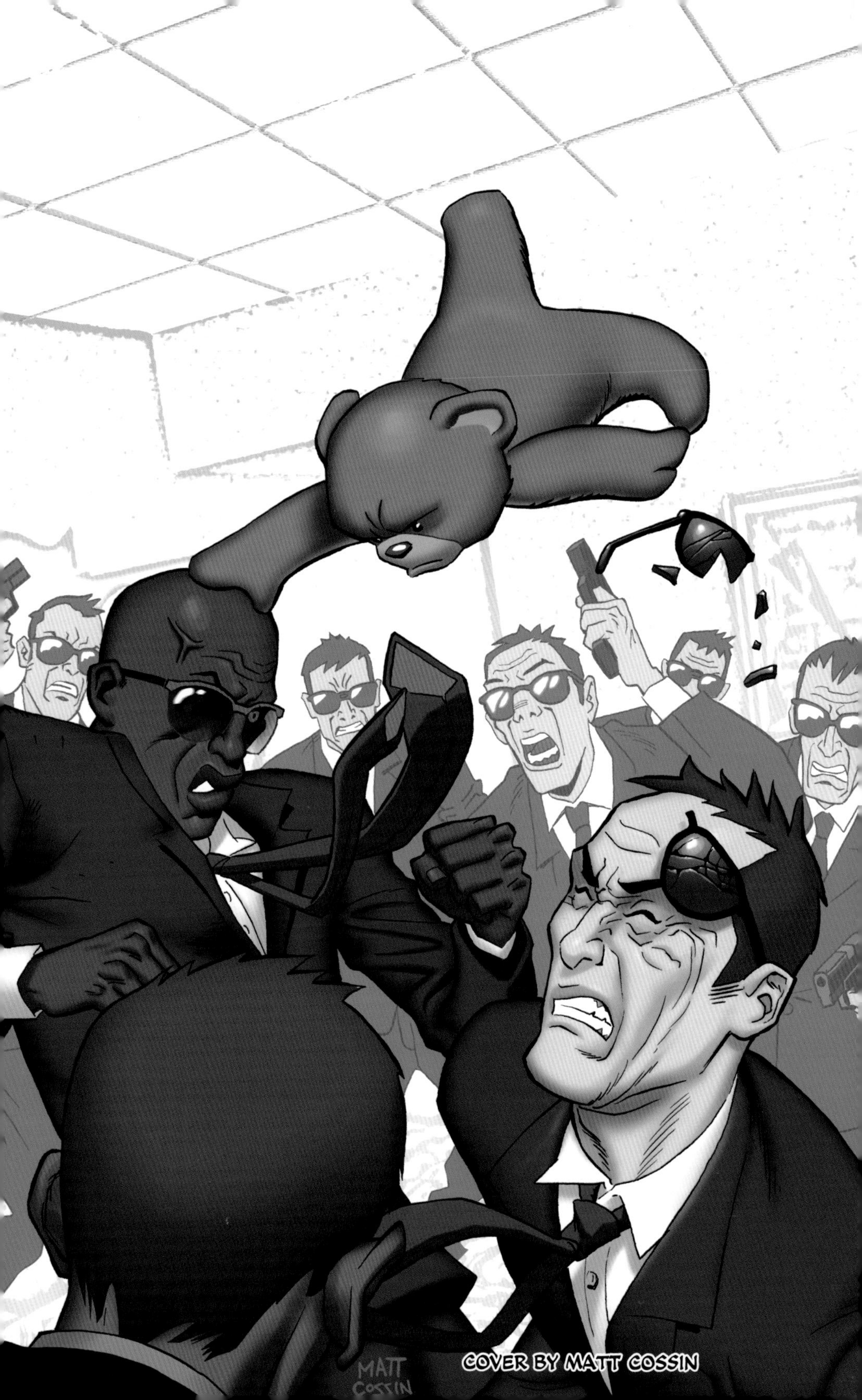
MATT
COSSIN

COVER BY MATT COSSIN

CHAPTER THREE

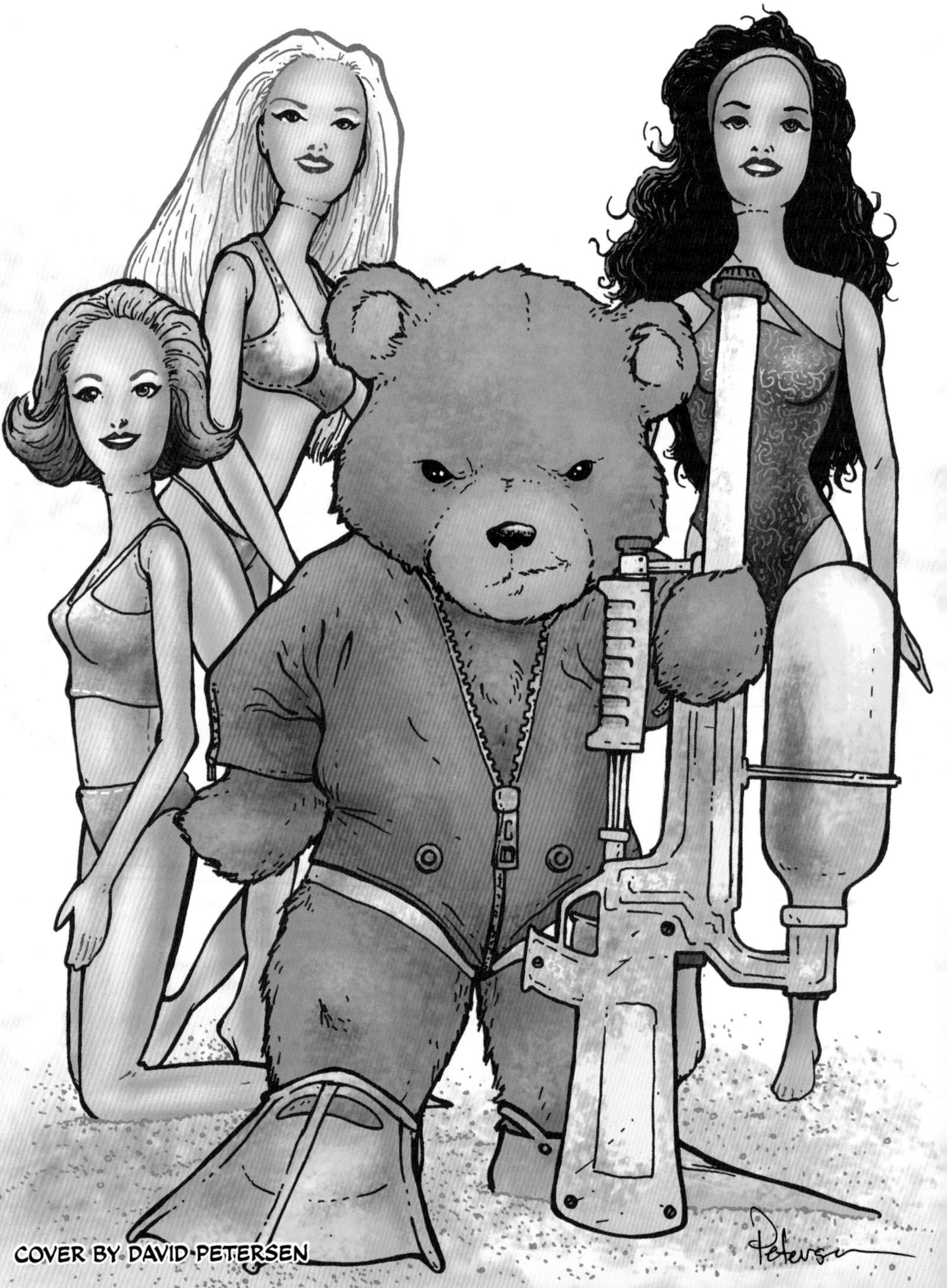

COVER BY DAVID PETERSEN

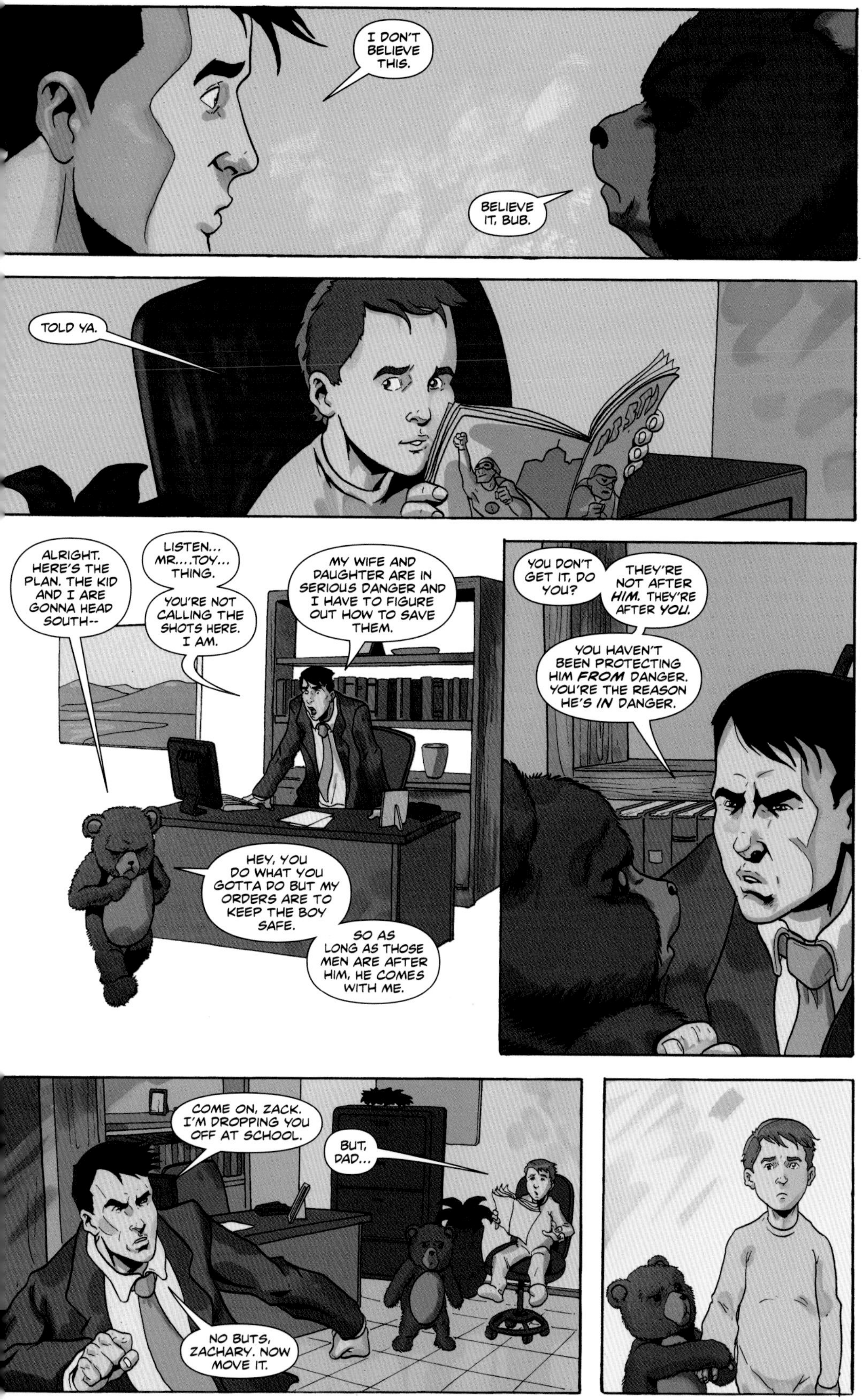

I DON'T BELIEVE THIS.
BELIEVE IT, BUB.
TOLD YA.
ALRIGHT. HERE'S THE PLAN. THE KID AND I ARE GONNA HEAD SOUTH--
LISTEN... MR....TOY... THING.
YOU'RE NOT CALLING THE SHOTS HERE. I AM.
MY WIFE AND DAUGHTER ARE IN SERIOUS DANGER AND I HAVE TO FIGURE OUT HOW TO SAVE THEM.
HEY, YOU DO WHAT YOU GOTTA DO BUT MY ORDERS ARE TO KEEP THE BOY SAFE.
SO AS LONG AS THOSE MEN ARE AFTER HIM, HE COMES WITH ME.
YOU DON'T GET IT, DO YOU?
THEY'RE NOT AFTER *HIM.* THEY'RE AFTER *YOU.*
YOU HAVEN'T BEEN PROTECTING HIM *FROM* DANGER. YOU'RE THE REASON HE'S *IN* DANGER.
COME ON, ZACK. I'M DROPPING YOU OFF AT SCHOOL.
BUT, DAD...
NO BUTS, ZACHARY. NOW MOVE IT.

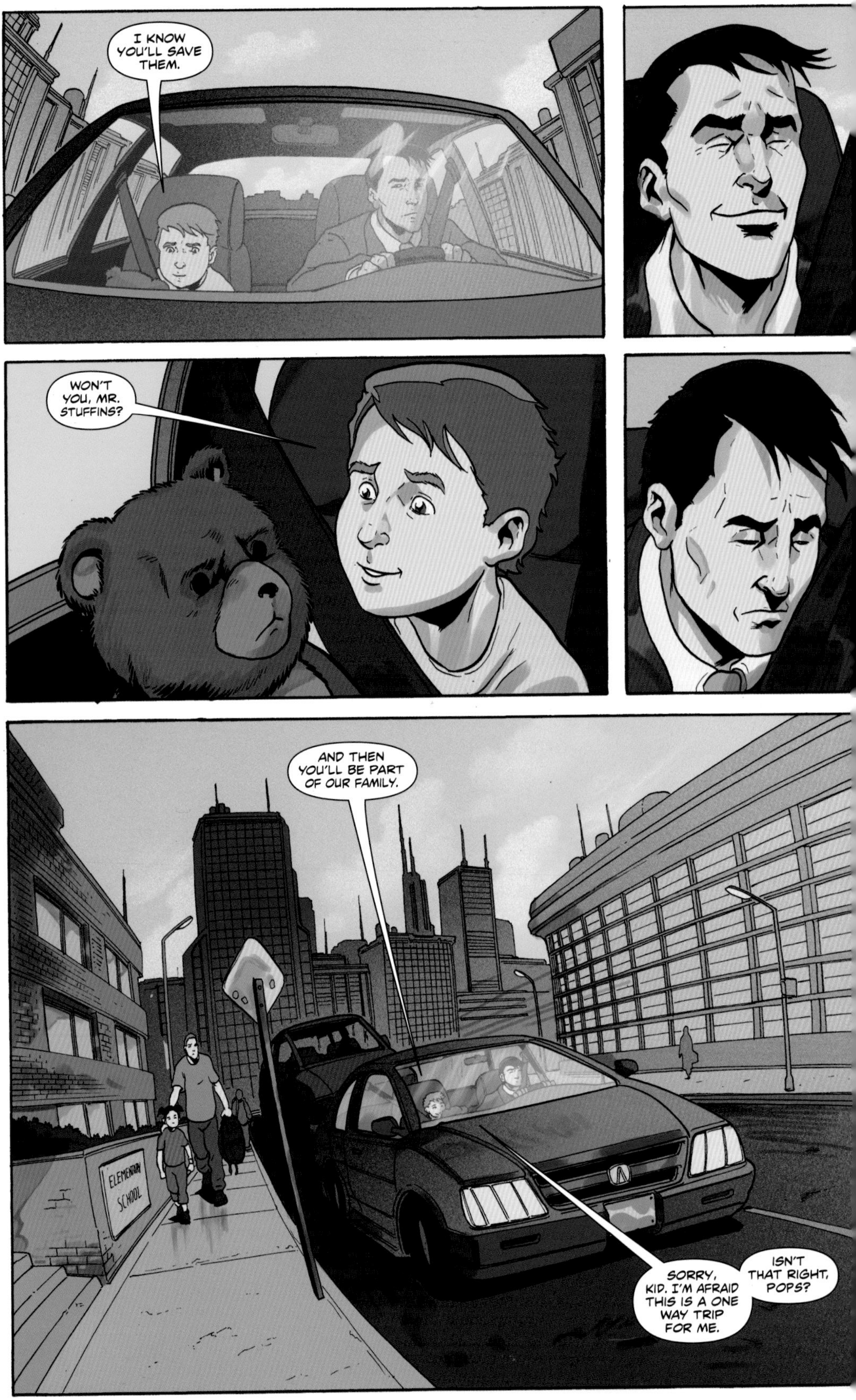

I KNOW YOU'LL SAVE THEM.
WON'T YOU, MR. STUFFINS?
AND THEN YOU'LL BE PART OF OUR FAMILY.
ISN'T THAT RIGHT, POPS?
SORRY, KID. I'M AFRAID THIS IS A ONE WAY TRIP FOR ME.
ELEMENTARY SCHOOL

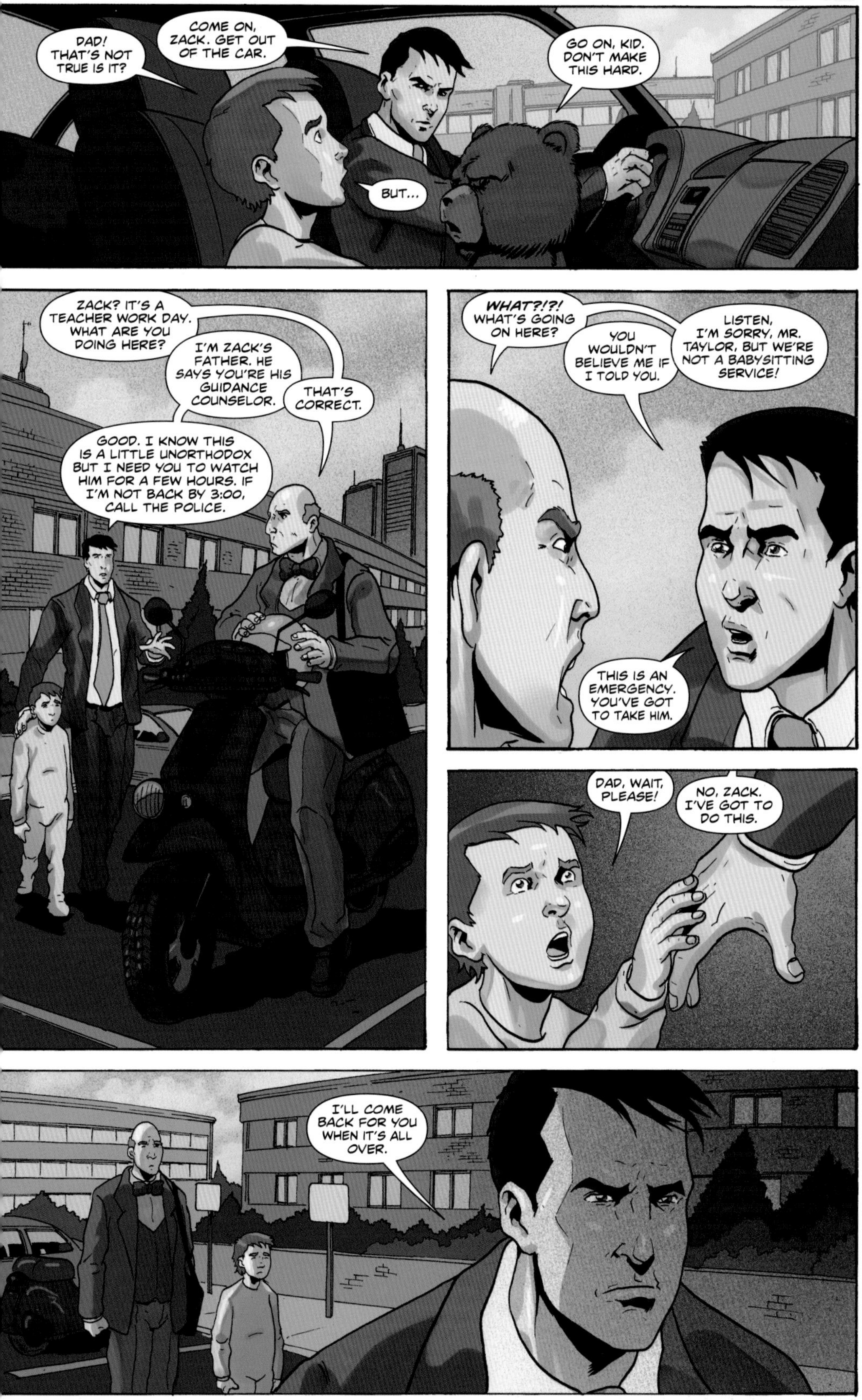
DAD! THAT'S NOT TRUE IS IT?
COME ON, ZACK. GET OUT OF THE CAR.
GO ON, KID. DON'T MAKE THIS HARD.
BUT...
ZACK? IT'S A TEACHER WORK DAY. WHAT ARE YOU DOING HERE?
I'M ZACK'S FATHER. HE SAYS YOU'RE HIS GUIDANCE COUNSELOR.
THAT'S CORRECT.
GOOD. I KNOW THIS IS A LITTLE UNORTHODOX BUT I NEED YOU TO WATCH HIM FOR A FEW HOURS. IF I'M NOT BACK BY 3:00, CALL THE POLICE.
WHAT?!?! WHAT'S GOING ON HERE?
YOU WOULDN'T BELIEVE ME IF I TOLD YOU.
LISTEN, I'M SORRY, MR. TAYLOR, BUT WE'RE NOT A BABYSITTING SERVICE!
THIS IS AN EMERGENCY. YOU'VE GOT TO TAKE HIM.
DAD, WAIT, PLEASE!
NO, ZACK. I'VE GOT TO DO THIS.
I'LL COME BACK FOR YOU WHEN IT'S ALL OVER.

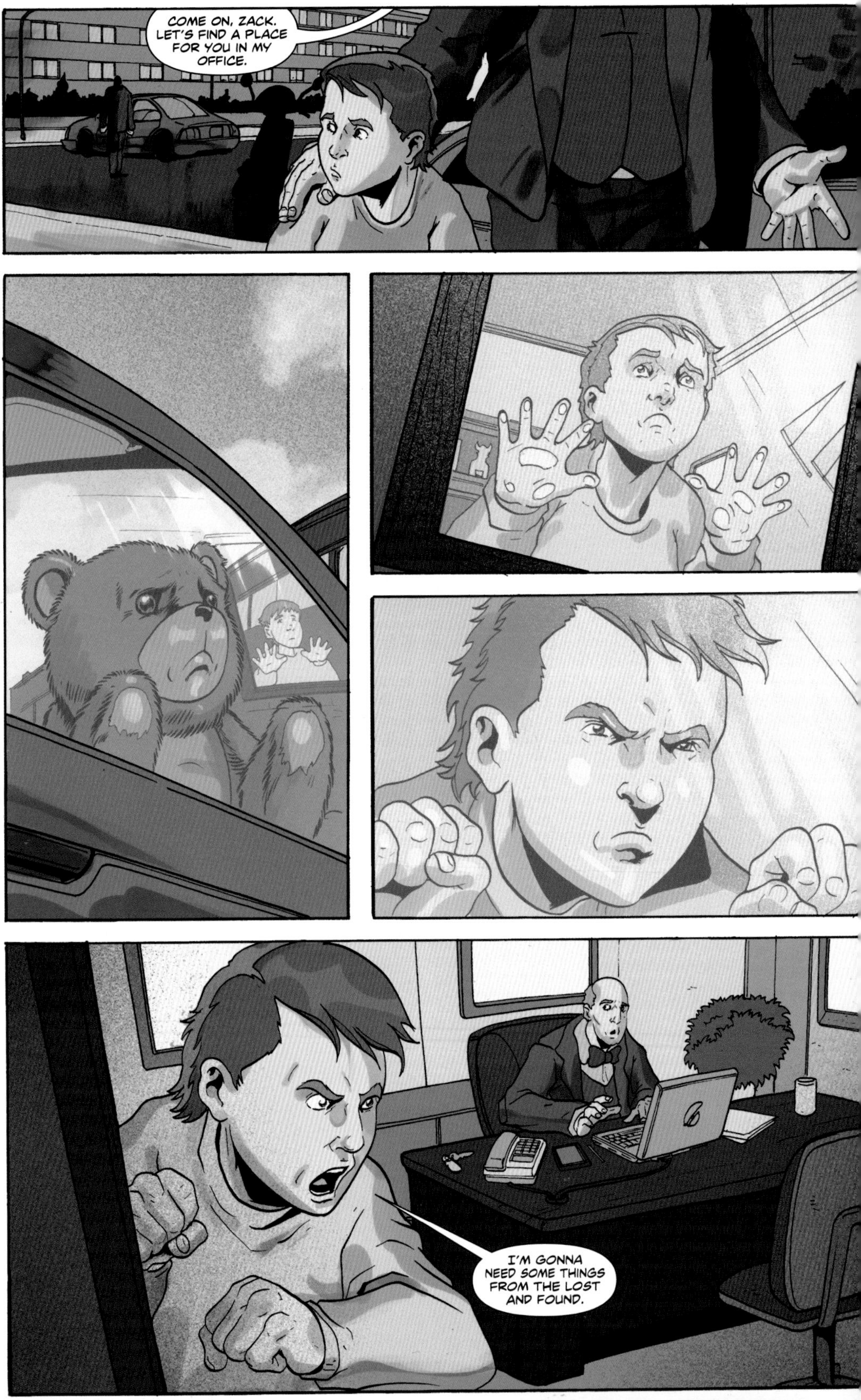
COME ON, ZACK. LET'S FIND A PLACE FOR YOU IN MY OFFICE.
I'M GONNA NEED SOME THINGS FROM THE LOST AND FOUND.

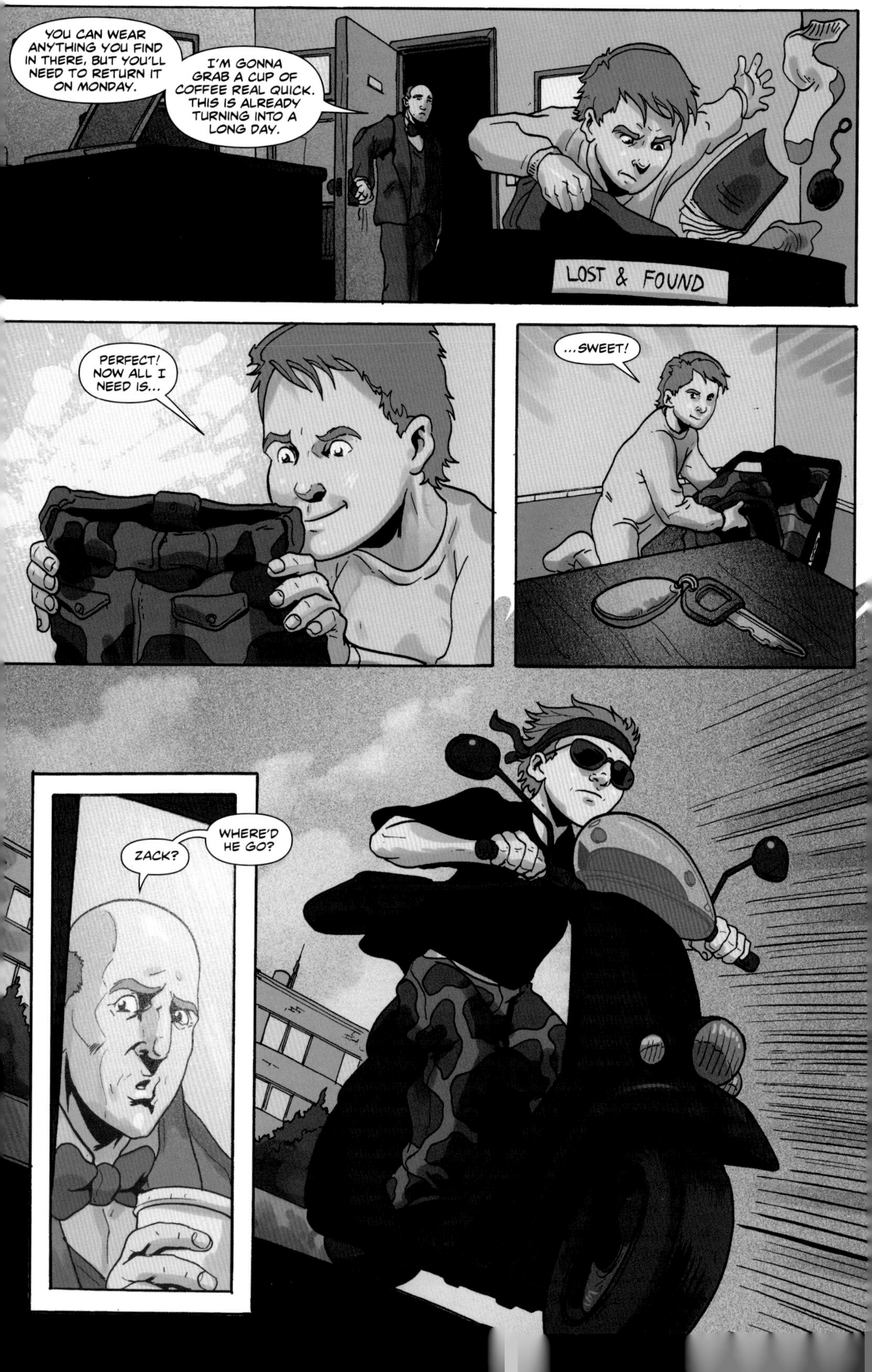
YOU CAN WEAR ANYTHING YOU FIND IN THERE, BUT YOU'LL NEED TO RETURN IT ON MONDAY.
I'M GONNA GRAB A CUP OF COFFEE REAL QUICK. THIS IS ALREADY TURNING INTO A LONG DAY.
LOST & FOUND
PERFECT! NOW ALL I NEED IS...
...SWEET!
ZACK?
WHERE'D HE GO?

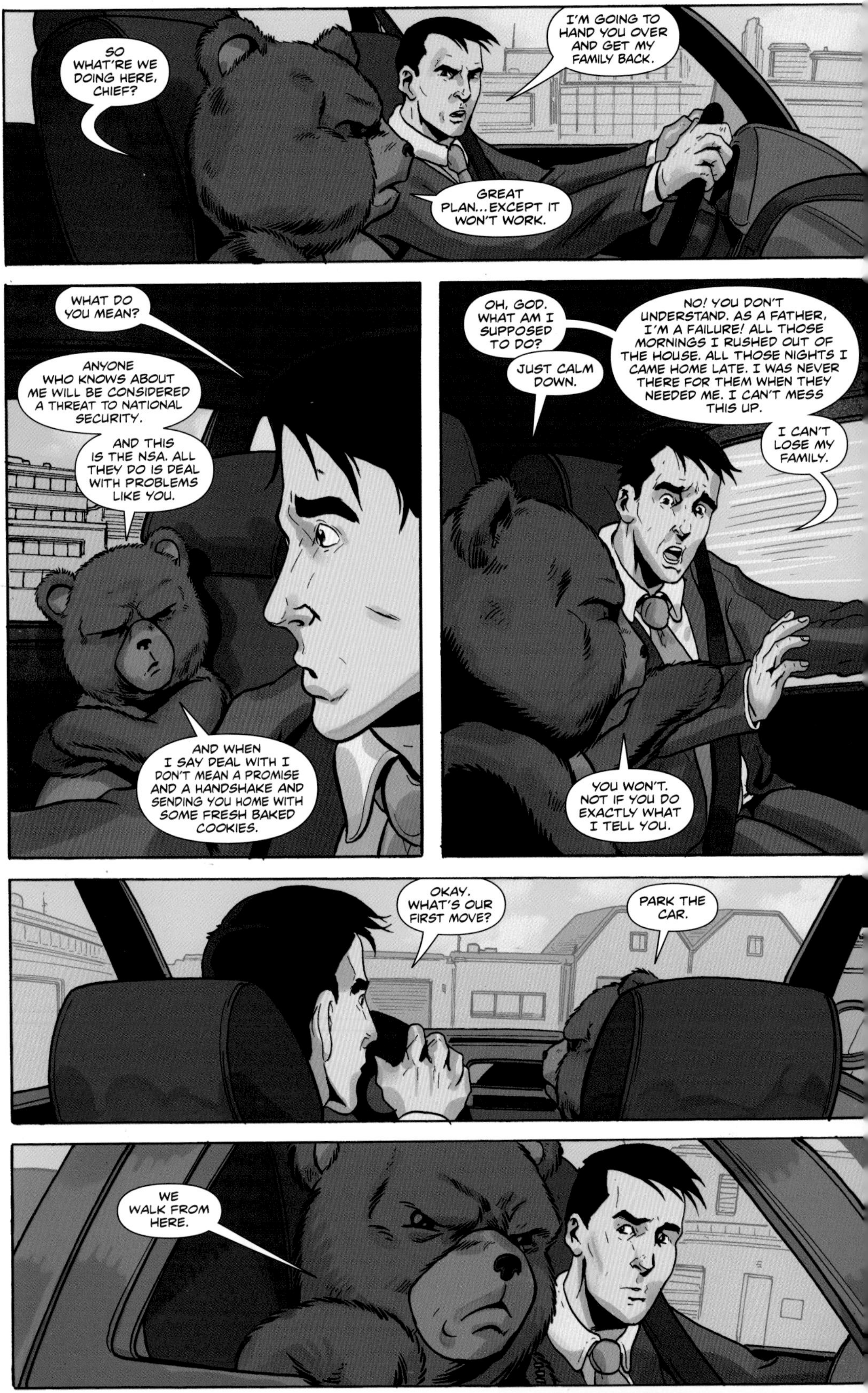
SO WHAT'RE WE DOING HERE, CHIEF?
I'M GOING TO HAND YOU OVER AND GET MY FAMILY BACK.
GREAT PLAN...EXCEPT IT WON'T WORK.
WHAT DO YOU MEAN?
ANYONE WHO KNOWS ABOUT ME WILL BE CONSIDERED A THREAT TO NATIONAL SECURITY.
AND THIS IS THE NSA. ALL THEY DO IS DEAL WITH PROBLEMS LIKE YOU.
AND WHEN I SAY DEAL WITH I DON'T MEAN A PROMISE AND A HANDSHAKE AND SENDING YOU HOME WITH SOME FRESH BAKED COOKIES.
OH, GOD. WHAT AM I SUPPOSED TO DO?
JUST CALM DOWN.
NO! YOU DON'T UNDERSTAND. AS A FATHER, I'M A FAILURE! ALL THOSE MORNINGS I RUSHED OUT OF THE HOUSE. ALL THOSE NIGHTS I CAME HOME LATE. I WAS NEVER THERE FOR THEM WHEN THEY NEEDED ME. I CAN'T MESS THIS UP.
I CAN'T LOSE MY FAMILY.
YOU WON'T. NOT IF YOU DO EXACTLY WHAT I TELL YOU.
OKAY. WHAT'S OUR FIRST MOVE?
PARK THE CAR.
WE WALK FROM HERE.

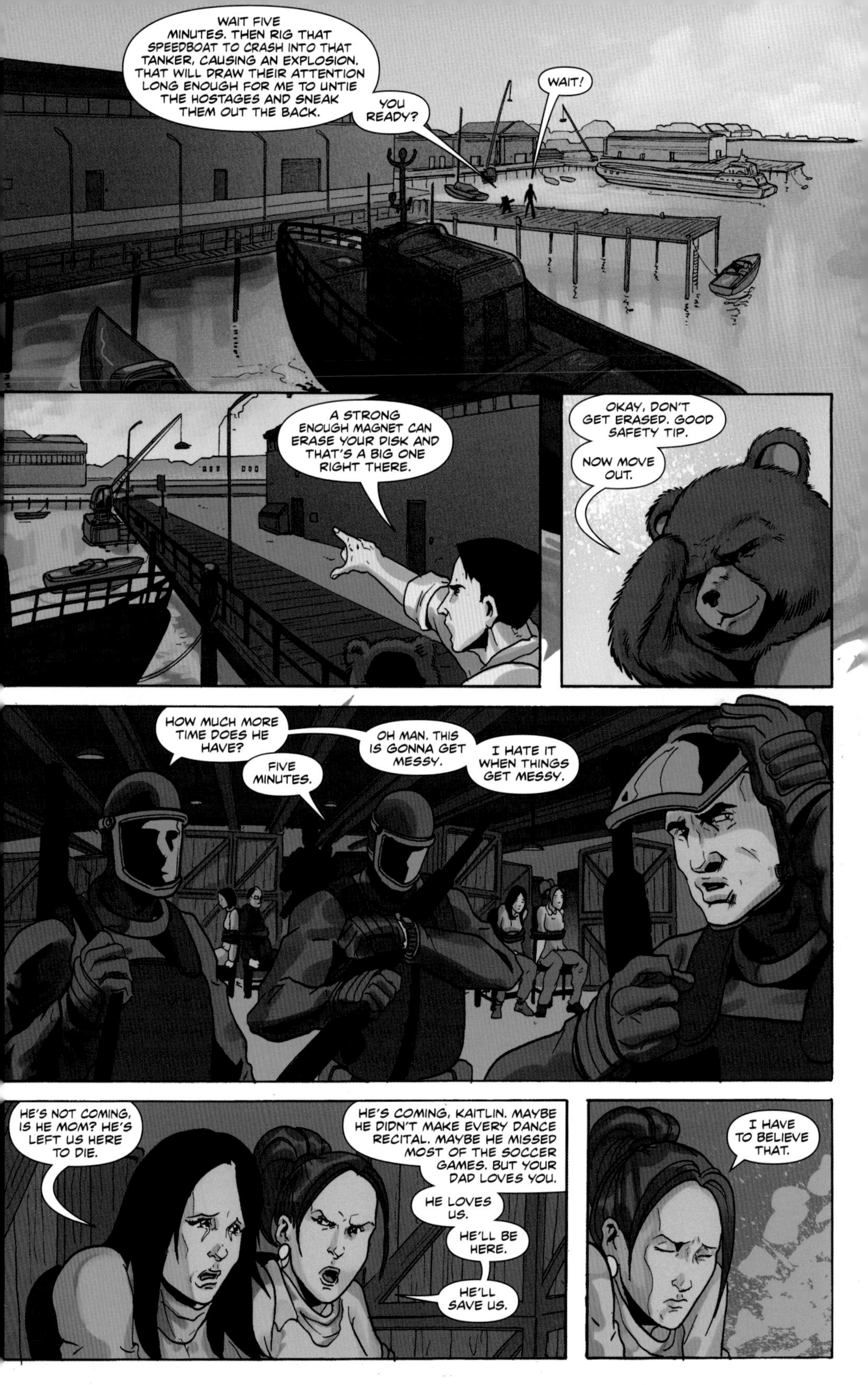
WAIT FIVE MINUTES. THEN RIG THAT SPEEDBOAT TO CRASH INTO THAT TANKER, CAUSING AN EXPLOSION. THAT WILL DRAW THEIR ATTENTION LONG ENOUGH FOR ME TO UNTIE THE HOSTAGES AND SNEAK THEM OUT THE BACK.
YOU READY?
WAIT!
A STRONG ENOUGH MAGNET CAN ERASE YOUR DISK AND THAT'S A BIG ONE RIGHT THERE.
OKAY, DON'T GET ERASED. GOOD SAFETY TIP.
NOW MOVE OUT.
HOW MUCH MORE TIME DOES HE HAVE?
FIVE MINUTES.
OH MAN. THIS IS GONNA GET MESSY.
I HATE IT WHEN THINGS GET MESSY.
HE'S NOT COMING, IS HE MOM? HE'S LEFT US HERE TO DIE.
HE'S COMING, KAITLIN. MAYBE HE DIDN'T MAKE EVERY DANCE RECITAL. MAYBE HE MISSED MOST OF THE SOCCER GAMES. BUT YOUR DAD LOVES YOU.
HE LOVES US.
HE'LL BE HERE.
HE'LL SAVE US.
I HAVE TO BELIEVE THAT.

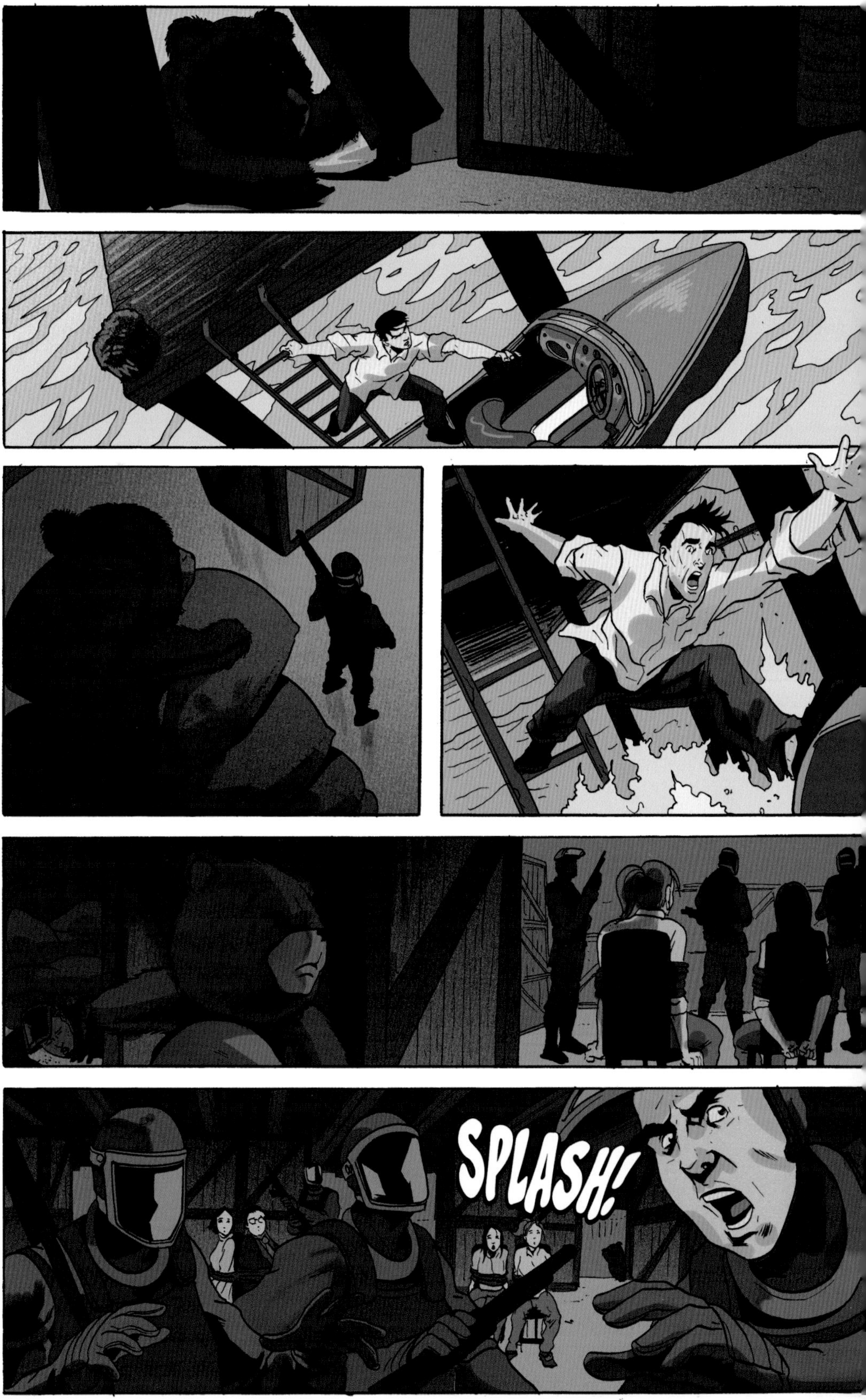
SPLASH!

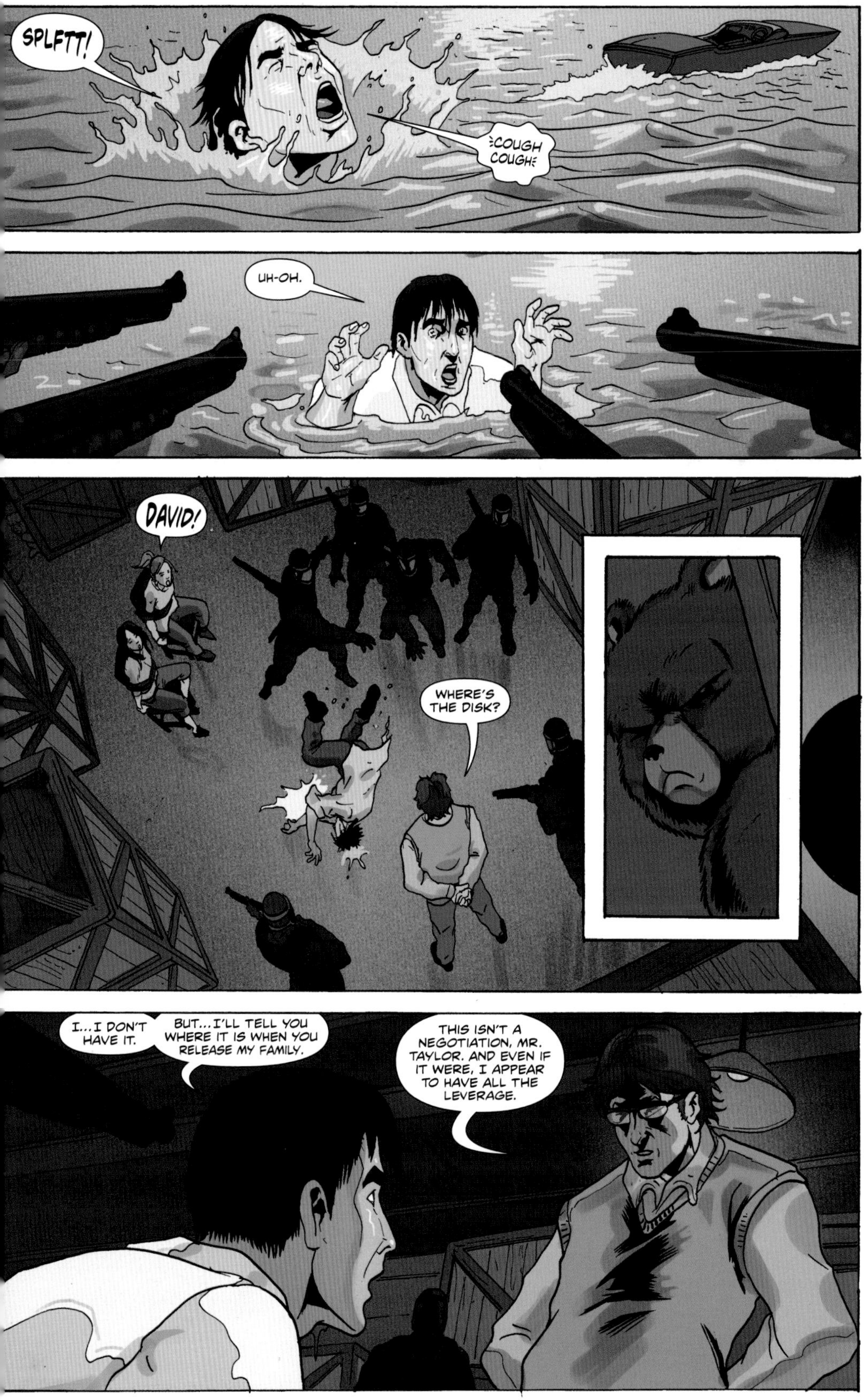
SPLFTT!
COUGH COUGH
UH-OH.
DAVID!
WHERE'S THE DISK?
I...I DON'T HAVE IT.
BUT...I'LL TELL YOU WHERE IT IS WHEN YOU RELEASE MY FAMILY.
THIS ISN'T A NEGOTIATION, MR. TAYLOR. AND EVEN IF IT WERE, I APPEAR TO HAVE ALL THE LEVERAGE.

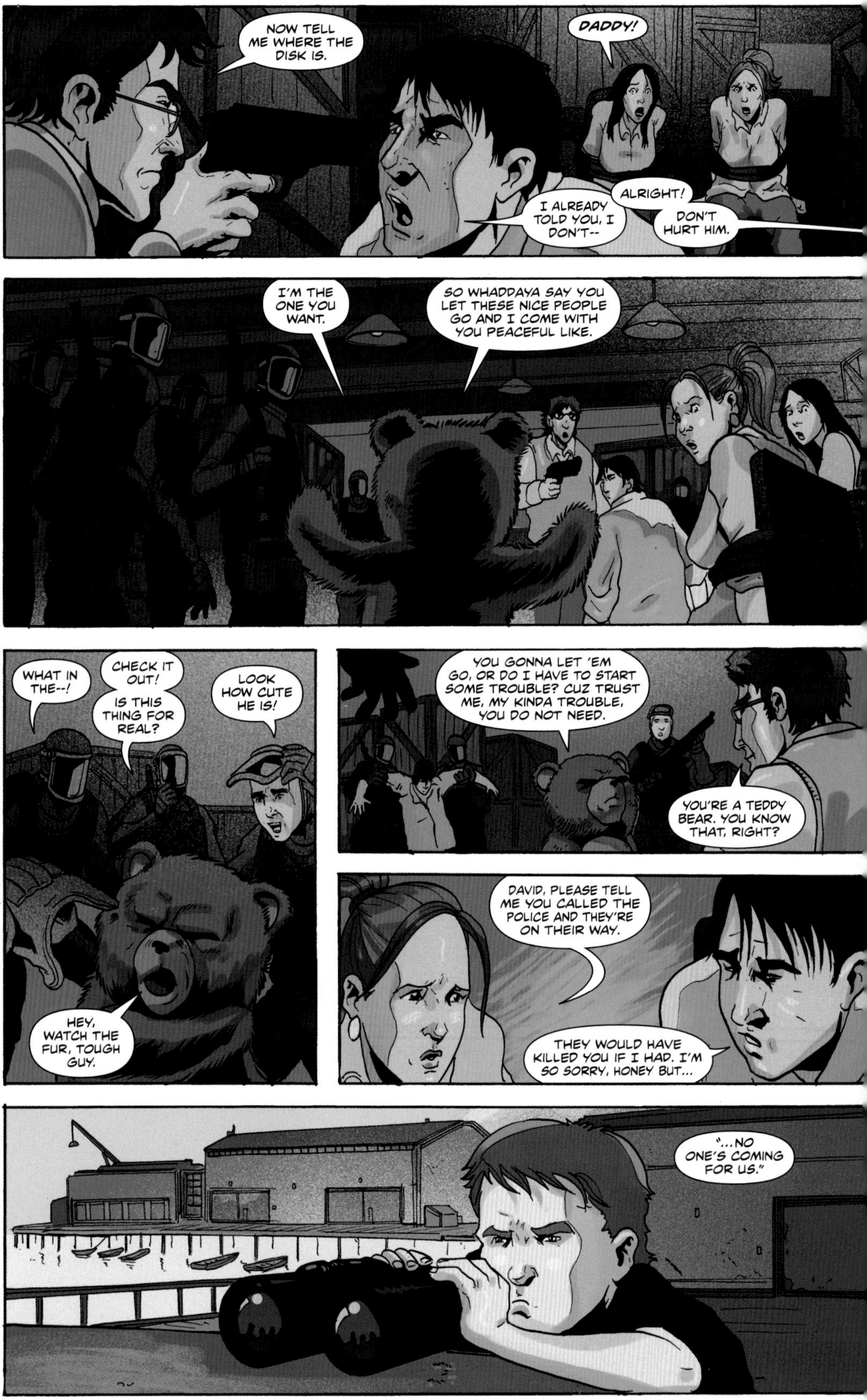
NOW TELL ME WHERE THE DISK IS.
DADDY!
I ALREADY TOLD YOU, I DON'T--
ALRIGHT!
DON'T HURT HIM.
I'M THE ONE YOU WANT.
SO WHADDAYA SAY YOU LET THESE NICE PEOPLE GO AND I COME WITH YOU PEACEFUL LIKE.
WHAT IN THE--!
CHECK IT OUT!
IS THIS THING FOR REAL?
LOOK HOW CUTE HE IS!
HEY, WATCH THE FUR, TOUGH GUY.
YOU GONNA LET 'EM GO, OR DO I HAVE TO START SOME TROUBLE? CUZ TRUST ME, MY KINDA TROUBLE, YOU DO NOT NEED.
YOU'RE A TEDDY BEAR. YOU KNOW THAT, RIGHT?
DAVID, PLEASE TELL ME YOU CALLED THE POLICE AND THEY'RE ON THEIR WAY.
THEY WOULD HAVE KILLED YOU IF I HAD. I'M SO SORRY, HONEY BUT...
"...NO ONE'S COMING FOR US."

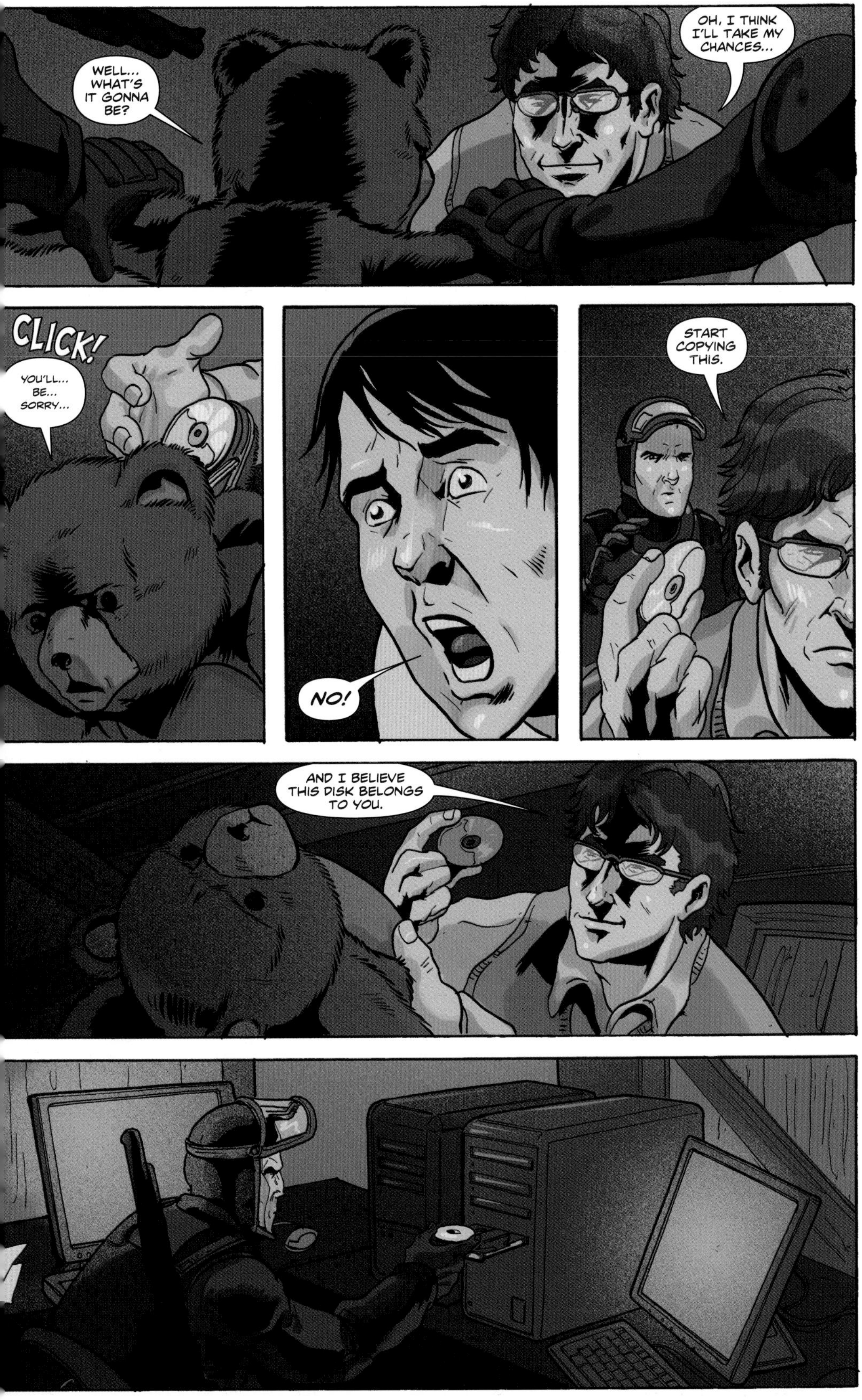
WELL... WHAT'S IT GONNA BE?
OH, I THINK I'LL TAKE MY CHANCES...
CLICK!
YOU'LL... BE... SORRY...
NO!
START COPYING THIS.
AND I BELIEVE THIS DISK BELONGS TO YOU.

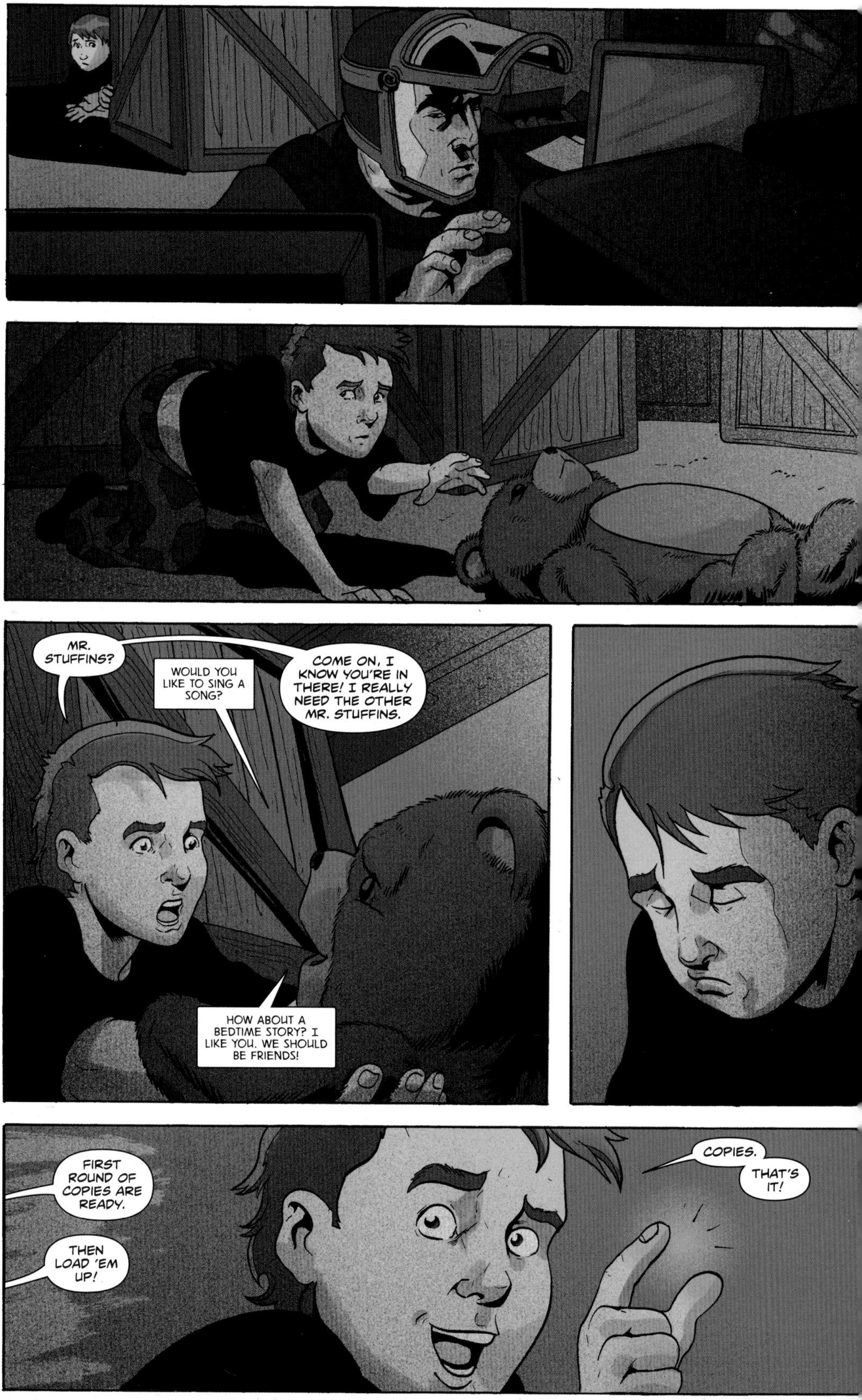
MR. STUFFINS?
WOULD YOU LIKE TO SING A SONG?
COME ON, I KNOW YOU'RE IN THERE! I REALLY NEED THE OTHER MR. STUFFINS.
HOW ABOUT A BEDTIME STORY? I LIKE YOU. WE SHOULD BE FRIENDS!
FIRST ROUND OF COPIES ARE READY.
THEN LOAD 'EM UP!
COPIES.
THAT'S IT!

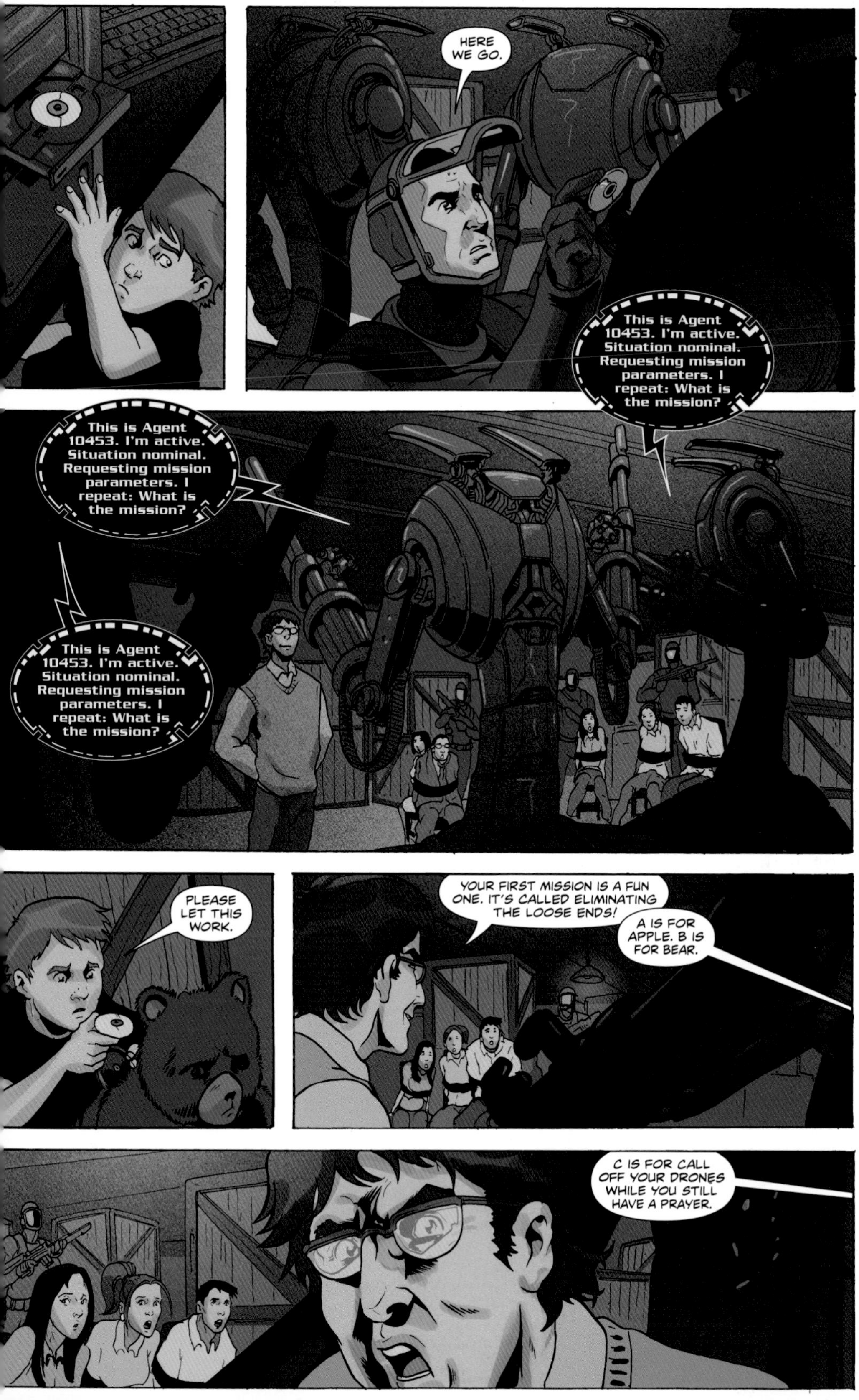
HERE WE GO.
This is Agent 10453. I'm active. Situation nominal. Requesting mission parameters. I repeat: What is the mission?
This is Agent 10453. I'm active. Situation nominal. Requesting mission parameters. I repeat: What is the mission?
This is Agent 10453. I'm active. Situation nominal. Requesting mission parameters. I repeat: What is the mission?
PLEASE LET THIS WORK.
YOUR FIRST MISSION IS A FUN ONE. IT'S CALLED ELIMINATING THE LOOSE ENDS!
A IS FOR APPLE. B IS FOR BEAR.
C IS FOR CALL OFF YOUR DRONES WHILE YOU STILL HAVE A PRAYER.

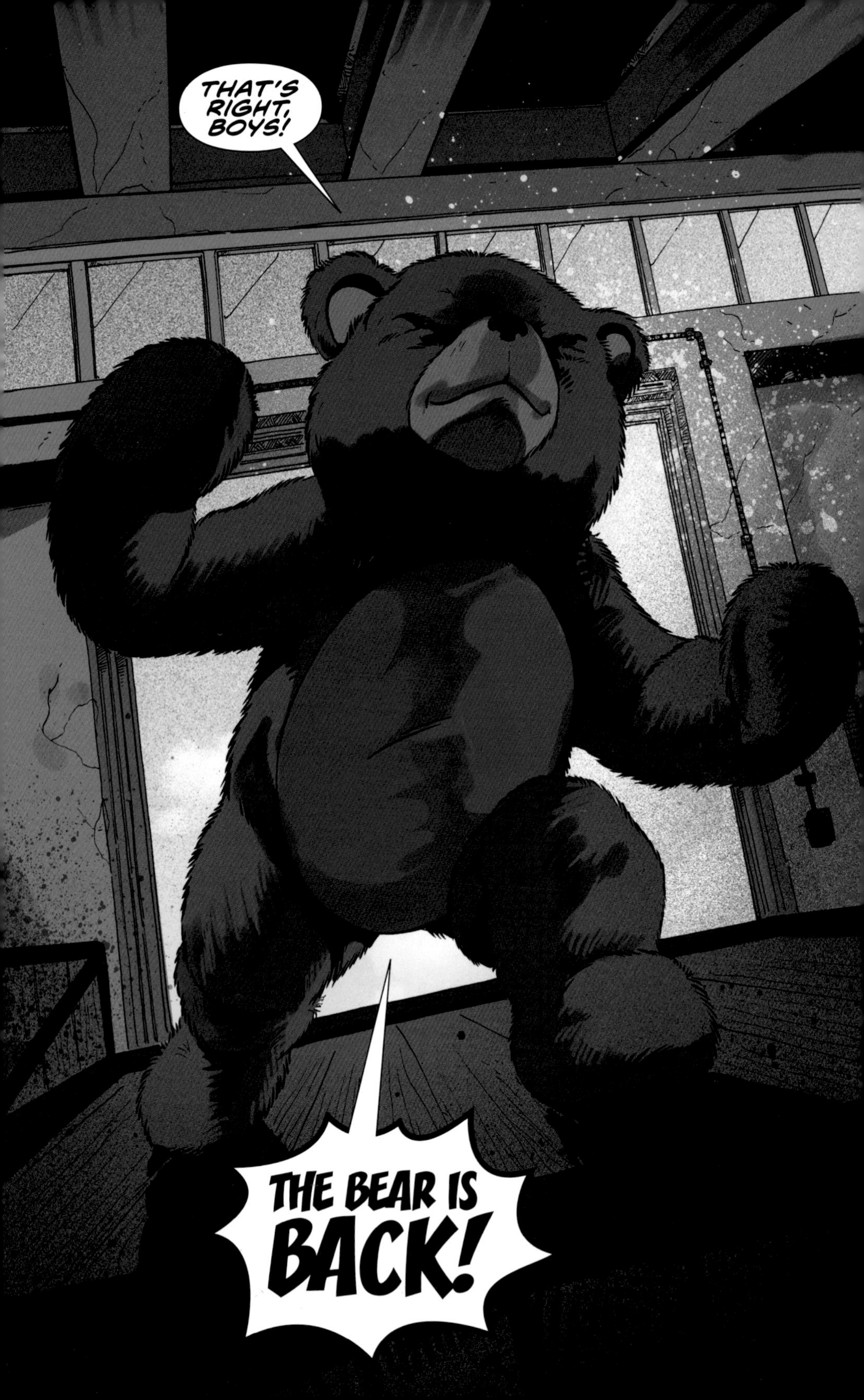
THAT'S RIGHT, BOYS!
THE BEAR IS BACK!

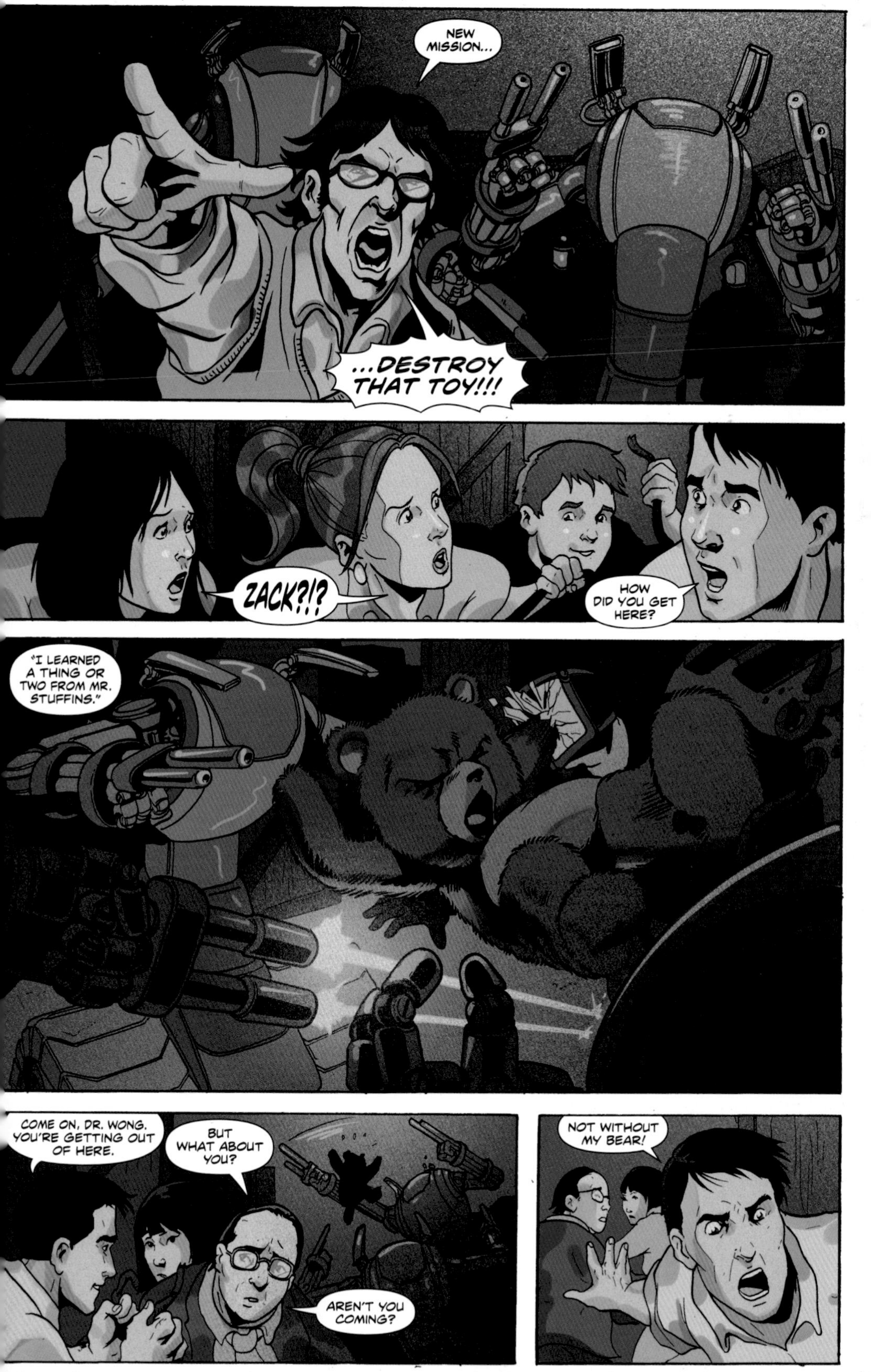
NEW MISSION...
...DESTROY THAT TOY!!!
ZACK?!?
HOW DID YOU GET HERE?
"I LEARNED A THING OR TWO FROM MR. STUFFINS."
COME ON, DR. WONG. YOU'RE GETTING OUT OF HERE.
BUT WHAT ABOUT YOU?
AREN'T YOU COMING?
NOT WITHOUT MY BEAR!

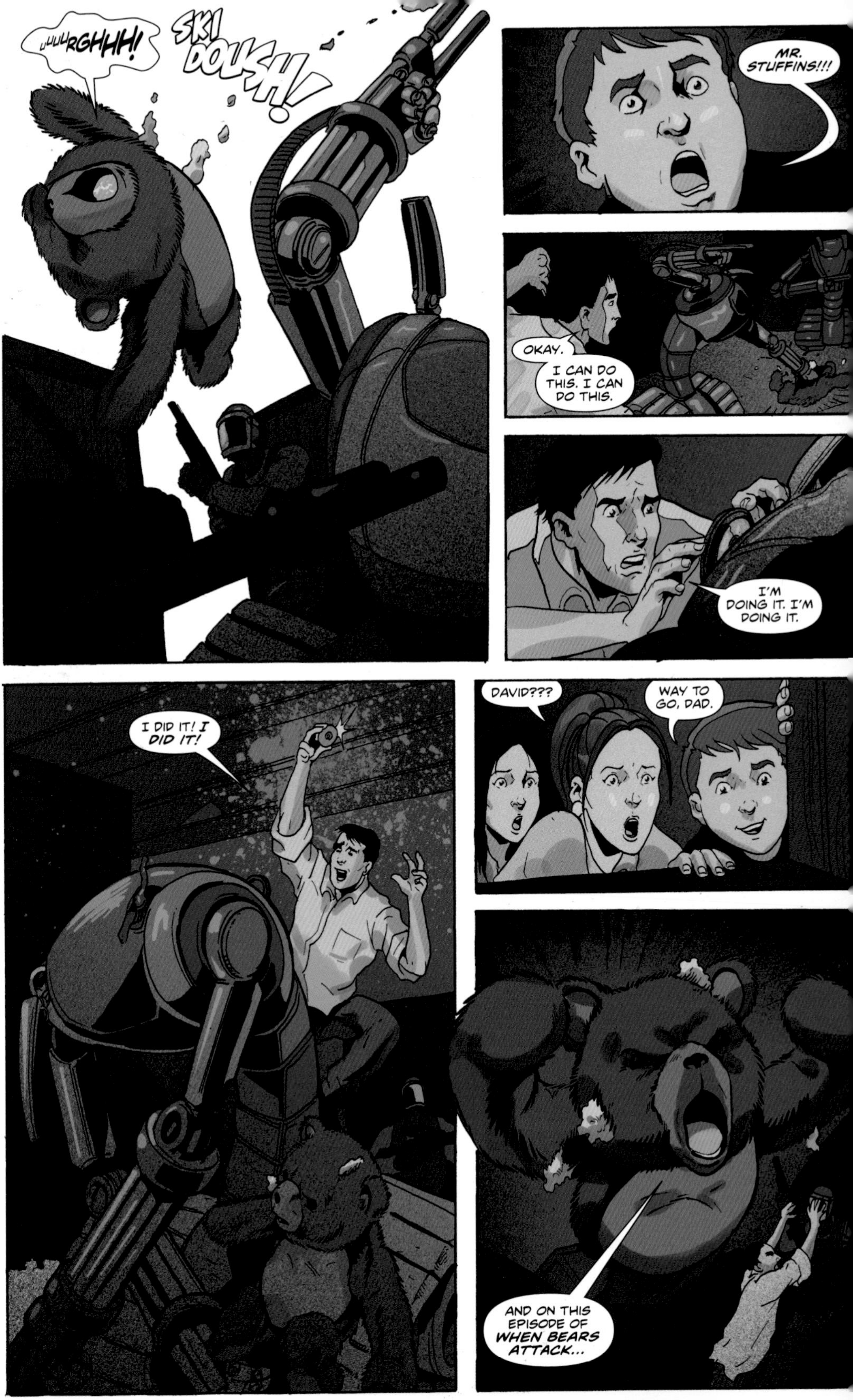
UUUURGHHH!
SKI DOUSH!
MR. STUFFINS!!!
OKAY.
I CAN DO THIS. I CAN DO THIS.
I'M DOING IT. I'M DOING IT.
I DID IT! I DID IT!
DAVID???
WAY TO GO, DAD.
AND ON THIS EPISODE OF WHEN BEARS ATTACK...

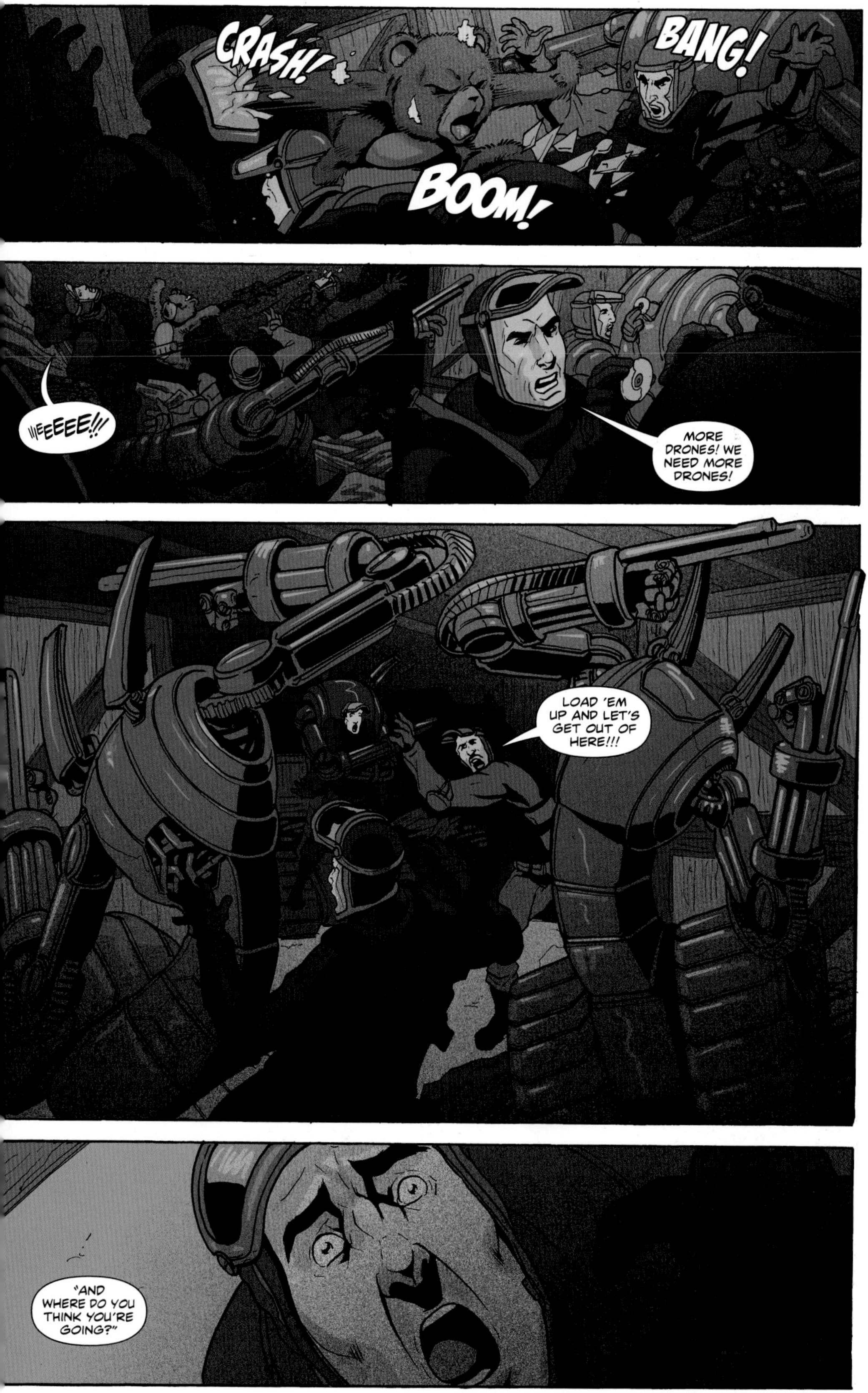
CRASH!
BANG!
BOOM!
IIIEEEEE!!!
MORE DRONES! WE NEED MORE DRONES!
LOAD 'EM UP AND LET'S GET OUT OF HERE!!!
"AND WHERE DO YOU THINK YOU'RE GOING?"

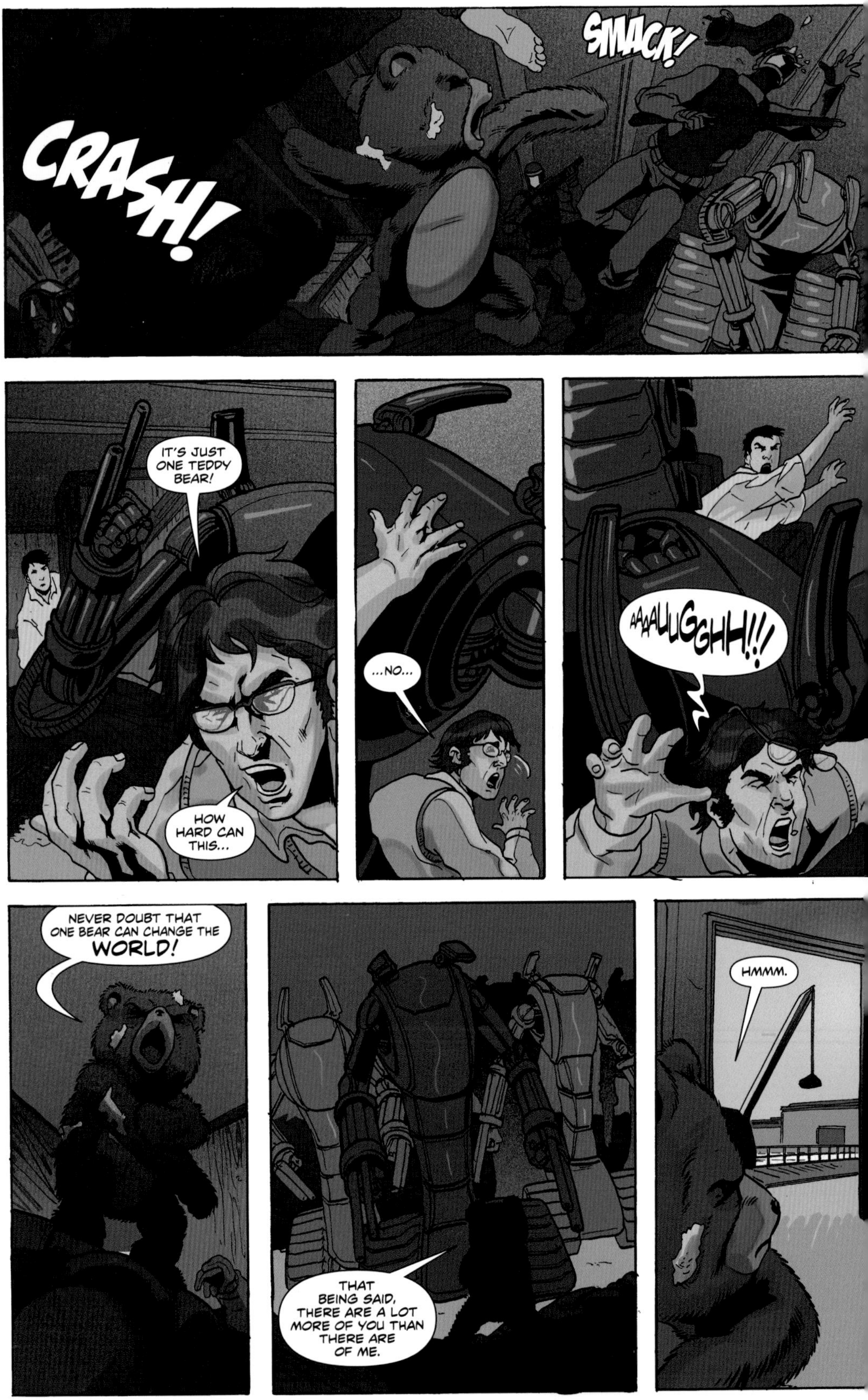
SMACK!
CRASH!
IT'S JUST ONE TEDDY BEAR!
HOW HARD CAN THIS...
...NO...
AAAAUUGGHH!!!
NEVER DOUBT THAT ONE BEAR CAN CHANGE THE WORLD!
THAT BEING SAID, THERE ARE A LOT MORE OF YOU THAN THERE ARE OF ME.
HMMM.

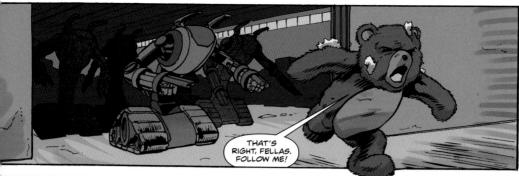

THAT'S RIGHT, FELLAS. FOLLOW ME!

IT'S DO OR DIE TIME.

DAD? WHAT'S HE DOING?

HE'S SAVING US, ZACK. JUST LIKE HE SAID HE WOULD.

NOO!

CLUNK

CLUNK

CLUNK

ZACK...

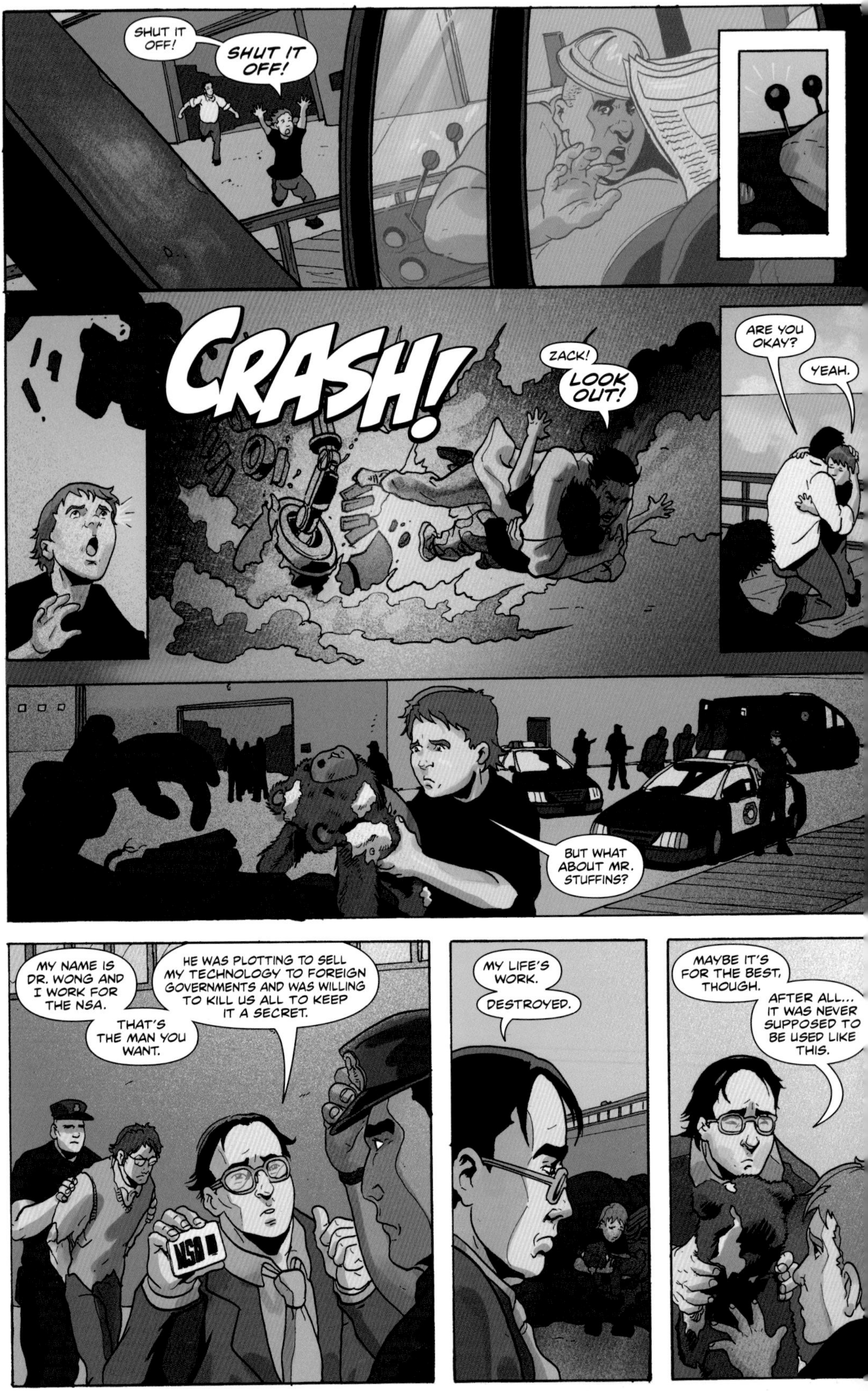
SHUT IT OFF!
SHUT IT OFF!
CRASH!
ZACK!
LOOK OUT!
ARE YOU OKAY?
YEAH.
BUT WHAT ABOUT MR. STUFFINS?
MY NAME IS DR. WONG AND I WORK FOR THE NSA.
THAT'S THE MAN YOU WANT.
HE WAS PLOTTING TO SELL MY TECHNOLOGY TO FOREIGN GOVERNMENTS AND WAS WILLING TO KILL US ALL TO KEEP IT A SECRET.
MY LIFE'S WORK.
DESTROYED.
MAYBE IT'S FOR THE BEST, THOUGH.
AFTER ALL... IT WAS NEVER SUPPOSED TO BE USED LIKE THIS.

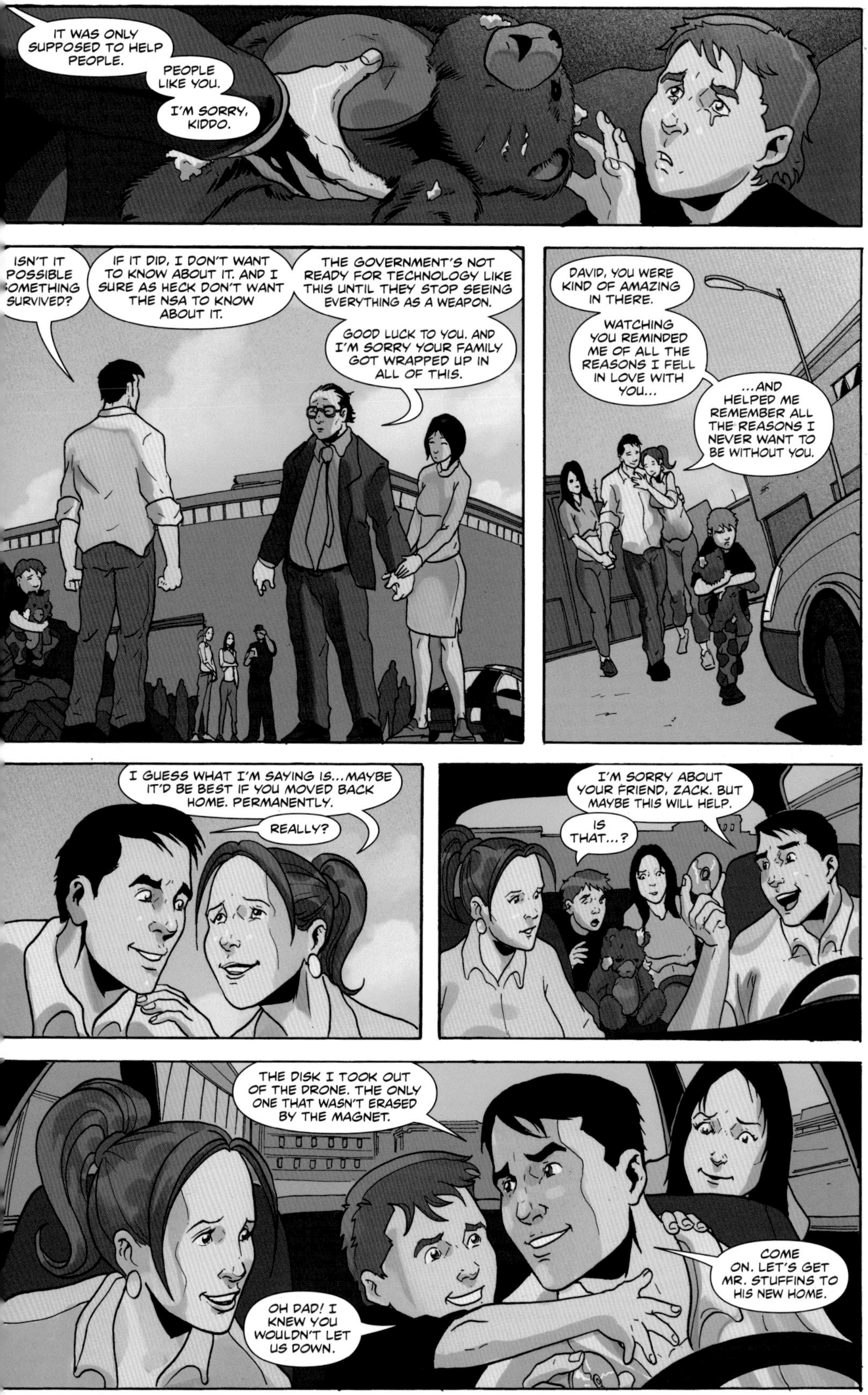
IT WAS ONLY SUPPOSED TO HELP PEOPLE.
PEOPLE LIKE YOU.
I'M SORRY, KIDDO.
ISN'T IT POSSIBLE SOMETHING SURVIVED?
IF IT DID, I DON'T WANT TO KNOW ABOUT IT. AND I SURE AS HECK DON'T WANT THE NSA TO KNOW ABOUT IT.
THE GOVERNMENT'S NOT READY FOR TECHNOLOGY LIKE THIS UNTIL THEY STOP SEEING EVERYTHING AS A WEAPON.
GOOD LUCK TO YOU. AND I'M SORRY YOUR FAMILY GOT WRAPPED UP IN ALL OF THIS.
DAVID, YOU WERE KIND OF AMAZING IN THERE.
WATCHING YOU REMINDED ME OF ALL THE REASONS I FELL IN LOVE WITH YOU...
...AND HELPED ME REMEMBER ALL THE REASONS I NEVER WANT TO BE WITHOUT YOU.
I GUESS WHAT I'M SAYING IS...MAYBE IT'D BE BEST IF YOU MOVED BACK HOME. PERMANENTLY.
REALLY?
I'M SORRY ABOUT YOUR FRIEND, ZACK. BUT MAYBE THIS WILL HELP.
IS THAT...?
THE DISK I TOOK OUT OF THE DRONE. THE ONLY ONE THAT WASN'T ERASED BY THE MAGNET.
OH DAD! I KNEW YOU WOULDN'T LET US DOWN.
COME ON. LET'S GET MR. STUFFINS TO HIS NEW HOME.

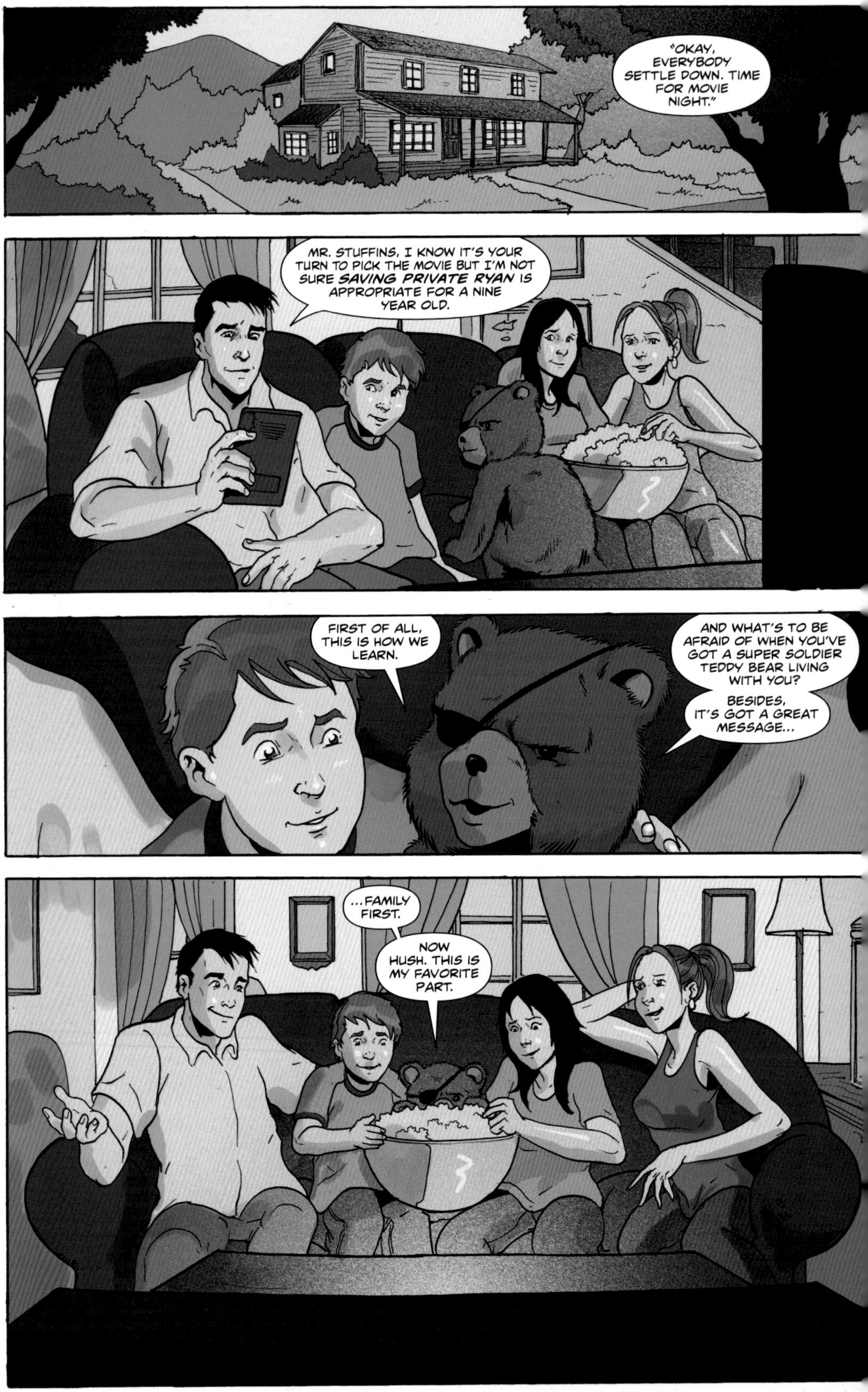
"OKAY, EVERYBODY SETTLE DOWN. TIME FOR MOVIE NIGHT."
MR. STUFFINS, I KNOW IT'S YOUR TURN TO PICK THE MOVIE BUT I'M NOT SURE SAVING PRIVATE RYAN IS APPROPRIATE FOR A NINE YEAR OLD.
FIRST OF ALL, THIS IS HOW WE LEARN.
AND WHAT'S TO BE AFRAID OF WHEN YOU'VE GOT A SUPER SOLDIER TEDDY BEAR LIVING WITH YOU?
BESIDES, IT'S GOT A GREAT MESSAGE...
...FAMILY FIRST.
NOW HUSH. THIS IS MY FAVORITE PART.

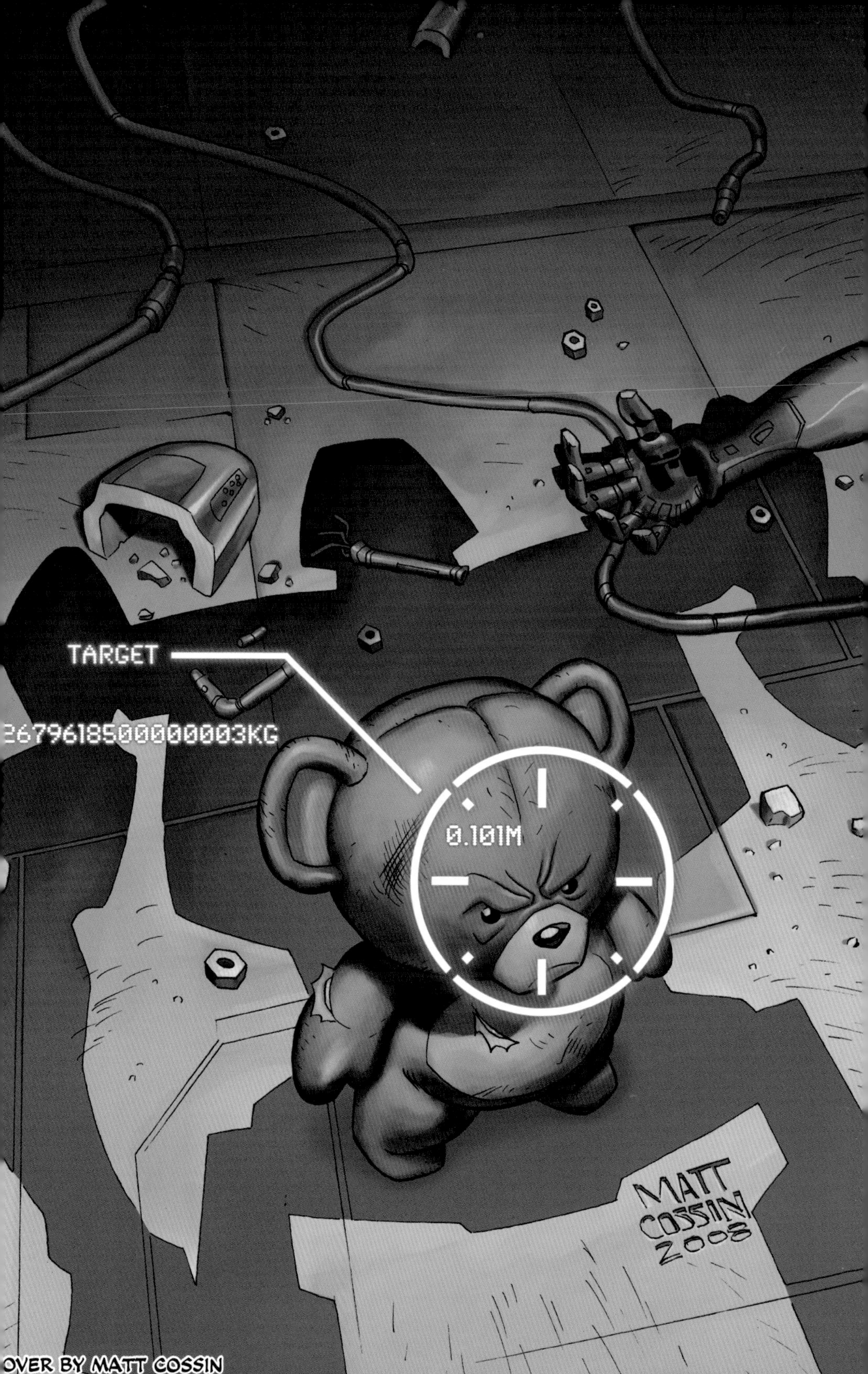
TARGET
267961850000000003KG
0.101M
MATT COSSIN 2008

OVER BY MATT COSSIN

CONFIDENTIAL

CONFIDENTIAL

MAY 20th, 2009

NATIONAL SECURITY ACTION MEMORANDUM NO. 4009

TO: The Secretary of State
The Secretary of Defense

SUBJECT: The Bear

Since the incident at the waterfront, the rogue agent known as "Mr. Stuffins" has been believed, by some in the department, to still be active. Originally it was thought that he could be found at [redacted], [redacted], and [redacted] (that last theory was disproven when it was realized that Stuffins would not ice skate).

After months of grueling research Mr. Stuffins's main source of communications were discovered (during a coffee break). Via the mysterious yet growing organization known as "Twitter" Stuffins has chronicled his latest adventures. More can be found at

http://www.twitter.com/MisterStuffins

CONFIDENTIAL

CONFIDENTIAL

—Mr. Stuffins #1 hits shelves on Wednesday, April 29th. Which is ironic, cuz I hit a guy with a shelf just last Wednesday. 8:25 AM Apr 28th from web

—Worried about swine flu. Can bears get swine flu? 8:26 AM Apr 28th from web

—You think commenting on Facebook is infuriating... try texting with paws from a Navy warship somewhere off the Coast of Somalia!!! 11:33 AM Apr 28th from web

—Salt water and batteries do not mix. 11:34 AM Apr 28th from web

—Some are above the law. None are above the paw. 1:22 PM Apr 28th from web

—Think I'm getting the hang of this twitter thing. Duct-taped pencils to my paws for typing. Question: how secure are these communications? 2:15 PM Apr 28th from web

—And seriously... what are the symptoms of swine flu? My ears itch. 2:18 PM Apr 28th from web

—Just got an e-mail that someone is "following me on Twitter." Big mistake. Gonna double back and see if I can't outflank him. 11:04 PM Apr 28th from web

—Watching SHADOW FORCE. It's like

MAN VS. WILD meets THE A-TEAM. Where've you been all my life? "I pity the fool!" 7:24 AM May 2nd from web

—That reminds me. I think I need a catch phrase... 7:25 AM May 2nd from web

—How's about something like, "Get stuffed!" 7:26 AM May 2nd from web

—Stuck in a ventilation shaft. Communications are down. Hope someone is receiving this. The buy went bad. Elvis has left the building. 8:15 AM May 4th from web

—To clarify: I am Elvis. I have left the building... or at least I'm trying to. They don't make ventilation shafts like they used to. 8:19 AM May 4th from web

—No opposable thumbs, she says! I'll have you know my thumbs can oppose anything you put in front of them! 7:31 PM May 4th from web

—Can you send pictures with this thing? I'd like to send Stokes a snapshot of me opposing this guy with my thumb. 7:36 PM May 4th from web

—Mister Stuffins is now following Major Spoilers on Twitter. Why? Because he outranks me. It's in my programming. 11:08 PM May 4th from web

—Batteries fully recharged and ready for another day. 9:33 AM May 5th from web

—Lots of back-chatter about this "Cinco De Mayo." I'm assuming it's some sort of rebel leader or Mexican drug lord. Looking into it. 9:39 AM May 5th from web

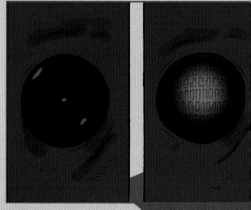

—At Home Depot. Have infiltrated a group of Mexican day laborers in an

attempt to find out more about the one they call Cinco De Mayo. 10:49 AM May 5th from web

—Did I mention I don't speak Spanish? It's become a problem. 2:14 PM May 5th from web

—Communication with the day laborers has broken down. I may have to resort to something less subtle. 2:17 PM May 5th from web

—Things are looking up. The one they call "Holmes" is leaving work early to meet Cinco De Mayo at a bar in Culver City. 3:14 PM May 5th from web

—Another dead end. Bar's packed -- must be some sort of holiday -- but still no sign of Cinco De Mayo. 3:53 PM May 5th from web

—The same name keeps coming up. Cerveza. Must be a Lieutenant in the organization. I'm close now. I can feel it. 4:34 PM May 5th from web

—Okay. On the run now. Things got a little out of hand at the bar. I really do need to learn Spanish. More when I reach the airport... 6:11 PM May 5th from web

—Cinco De Mayo's true identity remains a mystery. Still convinced whatever he's up to, it's big. All signs point to it going down today. 6:46 PM May 5th from web

—What am I missing? 6:47 PM May 5th from web

—How deep does this rabbit hole go? Have I inadvertently stumbled upon some kind of Mexican terrorist cell? Only one way to find out... 6:49 PM May 5th from web

—Have arrived at Los Angeles International Airport -- also known as LAX. Good name for the place. Security is a joke. 6:59 PM May 5th from web

—Handy travel tip #1: Do NOT tell a Japanese tourist to "take a picture, it'll last longer." It does not have the desired effect. 7:04 PM May 5th from web

—Finally. I've reached the Aeromexico Terminal. Gonna stow away in baggage. Sorry, Fluffy, your flight's been cancelled. 7:35 PM May 5th from web

—Mexico City, here I come. You can run Cinco De Mayo, but you cannot hide! 7:36 PM May 5th from web

—Landed last night. Had to find a place to recharge batteries... mine and the phone's. Back in action now. Will report again soon. 8:02 AM May 6th from web

—BTW, if you're shopping for a cat carrier, I recommend the Petmate Kennel Cab. Very comfortable... and extremely difficult to get out of. 8:07 AM May 6th from web

—Language barrier continues to be an obstacle. Adding "o" to the end of words not as effective as I'd hoped. 8:21 AM May 6th from web

—Mission update: available intel has led me to Mexico City in search of the mysterious Cinco De Mayo, whom I now believe to be a terrorist. 8:25 AM May 6th from web

—The name Cerveza keeps popping up, but only in back alleys and bars. His connection to Cinco De Mayo continues to elude me. 8:29 AM May 6th from web

—Seven hours scouring the streets of Mexico City and very little to show for it. 3:11 PM May 6th from web

—No one's talking. Or if they are, I have no idea what they're saying. Swiped a Spanish dictionary... but everything's written in Spanish. 3:14 PM May 6th from web

—People aren't talking about Cinco De Mayo, not a single mention in the last

7 hours, like he vanished overnight. I think they're scared. 3:18 PM May 6th from web

—Has he gone underground? Does he know I'm here? Part of me feels like I'm closer than ever. Another part feels like I missed something. 3:20 PM May 6th from web

—There's that name again, a new one -- Oso De Peluche. I keep hearing it everywhere I go. Oso this. Oso that. Oh so annoying! 3:23 PM May 6th from web

—An American cafe. I could ask them about Cinco De Mayo, but that's too obvious. That's exactly what he's expecting. Nice try, Cinco! 3:26 PM May 6th from web

—Even here, I can't seem to shake the feeling I'm deep in hostile territory. All eyes are on me. 3:32 PM May 6th from web

—Nothing in the news about a terrorist attack. I must have been wrong about this thing happening yesterday. I was so certain... 4:02 PM May 6th from web

—Lots of talk about the Swine Flu. News reports from all over Mexico. Signs of the quarantine being lifted. Is it over? I wonder... 4:09 PM May 6th from web

—THE SWINE FLU!! Of course! How could I be so blind? There has to be a connection. 4:12 PM May 6th from web

—Mission update: My hunt for Cinco De Mayo lead me to Mexico City, ground zero for the recent swine flu epidemic. Coincidence? Not likely. 4:15 PM May 6th from web

—This is a major breakthrough! Cinco De Mayo and the swine flu are connected. But how? A planned pandemic? What's their endgame? 4:41 PM May 6th from web

—It's go time! No more Mr. Nice Bear. 4:44 PM May 6th from web

—I can't alert the authorities, not until I have more. Twittering could be dangerous now, but what if something happens to me? 4:50 PM May 6th from web

—If you're receiving this... and then stop receiving it... you know... for like a long time... tell the world my story. 4:52 PM May 6th from web

—Back on the streets. No one talking about Cinco De Mayo. I'm convinced he's gone to ground. Or perhaps he's gone somewhere else...5:07 PM May 6th from web

—Swine flu has rooted itself in communities across the U.S., making containment impossible. 57 cases in Spain. 27 in the U.K....5:14 PM May 6th from web

—Potential global pandemic. Starting in Mexico City. Orchestrated by Cinco De Mayo? It's the only thing that makes sense.5:21 PM May 6th from web

—Totally off topic... a dog just peed on me. At least I think it's a dog.5:24 PM May 6th from web

—Seriously. I'm just standing here minding my own business, and it decides to do its business all over my leg. Not cool.5:25 PM May 6th from web

—Local pig farmers celebrating someone's birthday. Gonna use the party as cover. Get close to them. Find out what they know.5:51 PM May 6th from web

—Quick question... Is Mexican food in Mexico still Mexican food? Or is it just food?6:35 PM May 6th from web

—Party is in full swing now. Lots of kids running around. Singing. Dancing. Very festive. Almost easy to forget why I'm here.6:39 PM May 6th from web

—Birthday boy is here, blindfolded. Some sort of game? Look, there's another bear. Cute little fella, colorful. Maybe I can... OH DEAR GOD!!!6:50 PM May 6th from web

—Horrifying! I tried to stop it, but it happened so fast. They strung him up and beat him with sticks until he exploded! SAVAGES!7:10 PM May 6th from web

—That poor little bear. So brave. He never cried out. Even when they descended on him like locusts. Why must the innocent always suffer?7:13 PM May 6th from web

—On the move again. Anywhere but here. Hiding in the back of a truck headed for Tijuana. Who knows what new horrors await me there?7:27 PM May 6th from web

—I smell like dog pee.7:28 PM May 6th from web

—At last. I've reached Tijuana. Batteries are dangerously low. Must recharge.7:36 AM May 8th from web

—It's been days since the last mention of the one they call Cinco De Mayo. Always one step ahead of me.7:39 AM May 8th from web

—I still smell like dog pee. Gonna find a place to clean up and head back across the border.7:39 AM May 8th from web

—Only been here a short while, but can already tell this is Cerveza's town. His name is everywhere, on the lips of everyone. Local Warlord?7:42 AM May 8th from web

—The events of Mexico City have have shaken me to my core. I've seen things no bear should have to see. This is a dark place.7:49 AM May 8th from web

—On the plus side, I've found a water hose and can finally wash off the dog urine. Every cloud...7:51 AM May 8th from web

—While washing up, I found "Made in Taiwan" stamped on the bottom of my left foot. Getting back across the border is gonna be tricky.8:05 AM May 8th from web

—Mission update: Still no sign of Cinco De Mayo. Am now in Tijuana tracking swine flu, which I believe to be Mexican terrorist threat.8:07 AM May 8th from web

—Names of interest: Cinco De Mayo. Cerveza. Oso De Peluche.8:09 AM May 8th from web

—Thoughts growing fuzzy. Battery light blinking furiously. Recharging has become a priority.8:10 AM May 8th from web

—Stuffins is back, baby! Got my charge on and am ready for action!11:33 AM May 8th from web

—Mission update: My search for Cinco De Mayo has reached a dead end. Heading back across the border into the U.S.11:35 AM May 8th from web

—Repatriation is gonna be difficult. "Made in Taiwan" stamp on my left foot has forced me to consider an alternate route back into the U.S.11:37 AM May 8th from web

—My presence in Mexico can't have gone unnoticed. The name Oso De Peluche haunts my every step. The hunter has become the hunted.11:39 AM May 8th from web

—There are more Americans here, but I can't risk getting them involved.11:39 AM May 8th from web

–Language barrier continues to present an obstacle. Tried to get information in a bar - ended up having tequila poured down my throat.11:42 AM May 8th from web

–Found a local who speaks some broken english. He tells me my best chance to make it across the border is to find a coyote.11:45 AM May 8th from web

–Mission update: Looking for a coyote willing to sneak me across the border. I don't have any money, so this could get tricky.12:31 PM May 8th from web

–Hmm...all this time I thought a "churro" was a small burrowing rodent. Those signs in amusement parks make a lot more sense now.12:43 PM May 8th from web

–Overheard swine flu joke, something about Kermit's death and Miss Piggy being responsible. I don't get it. Kermit's not really dead, is he?12:47 PM May 8th from web

–I've been trying to talk to this coyote for hours, and all I've got to show for it is a handful of bite marks and more pee on my leg.7:02 PM May 8th from web

–Gave up on the coyote. Luckily I found some nice gentlemen with a plane who offered me a ride. And all I have to do is carry this package.8:31 PM May 8th from web

–Will Twitter again once I'm back in the loving arms of Mother America.8:32 PM May 8th from web

—I'm not dead folks, just tired. So very tired.10:52 AM May 17th from web

—You know how they say "don't drink the water" when you go to Mexico. well, same goes for using their batteries.10:53 AM May 17th from web

—Is it just me, or does RETURN OF THE JEDI catch too much flak because o the Ewoks? Feels like a subtle form of racism.12:43 PM May 17th from web

CONFIDENTIAL

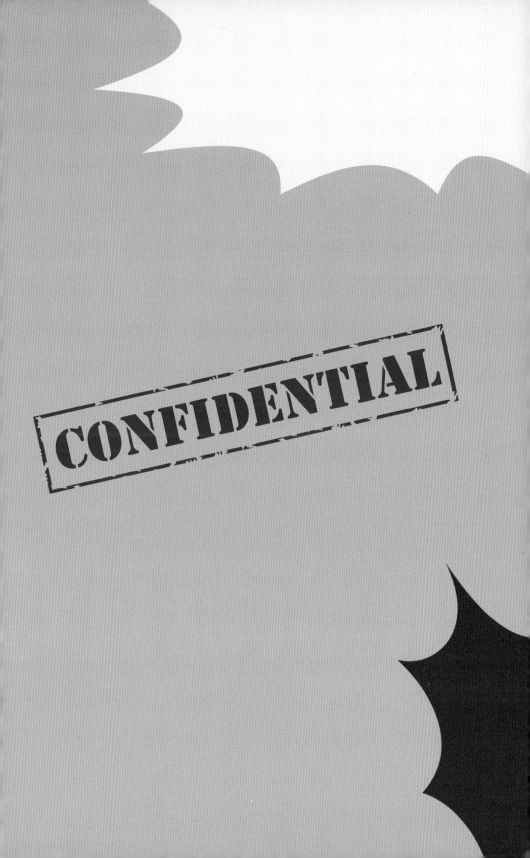

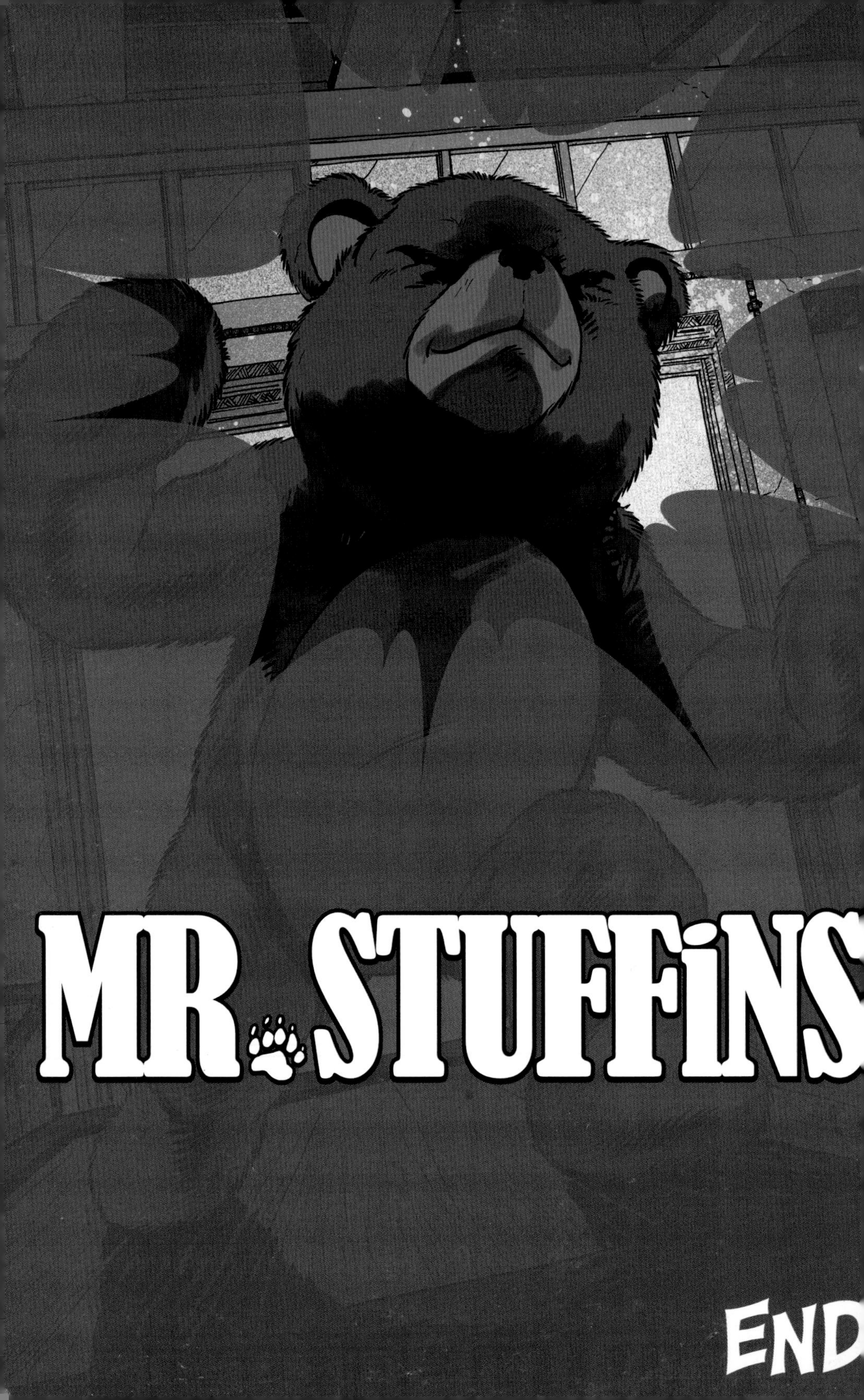
MR. STUFFINS
END